What people are

The Effective Presenter

Ryan's teachings have made me a significantly better public speaker and presenter. His advice on delivery and content structure has been enormously helpful. He has a unique ability to organize and map out the most meaningful content for audiences. I find myself referencing the lessons from this book in advance of every speaking engagement, no matter how large or small. His book contains everything you need to maximize your success in your next high-stakes presentation. It's definitely a must read!

Edward Wu, Serial Entrepreneur - Co-founder & CTO, Side Inc., Co-founder & former CTO, Vidyard

I spend my entire life dedicated to continuously improving my presentation skills as a tenured professor and professional speaker. It is for this exact reason that Warriner's book has a prominent position on my bookshelf. His framework of foundation, design, delivery and polishing is simple to understand. Most importantly, it's effective! Go ahead and read this book so you can make a significant positive impact on your next presentation. Your audience will thank you!

Dr. Nick Bontis, Professional Keynote Speaker, Award Winning Business Professor, DeGroote School of Business, McMaster University

No one is born a great presenter. Presenting effectively is a learned skill. Warriner's book is a clear guide to enhancing your skill level. It outlines the necessary techniques to strengthen your speaking confidence forever!

Mark Bowden, Body Language Expert, Professional Speaker, Co-founder & President, TRUTHPLANE

Ryan Warriner's framework turns hesitation and best guesses into confidence and success. After reading his book, my presentations have been easier to deliver, and have left greater impact on my audiences. The readability of Ryan's conversational style helps his lessons to stick and perpetually add value to your presentation. His book is a must read for anyone who has ever approached a presentation otherwise!

David J. Hill, Director of Financial Planning, Dentsu Aegis Network, former Director of Finance, Toronto Blue Jays

In the past, I would dread the day of my presentation. I remember being concerned throughout the entire day, before presenting in a meeting. After reading Ryan's book, I feel energized and enthusiastic in advance of my presentations. I'm now equipped with the knowledge and confidence to ace any speaking occasion. I highly recommend this book for anyone who presents or speaks in their role.

Bryan Eyler, Senior Software Engineer, Google

This is an amazingly enjoyable read with the perfect combination of meaningful insight, substance, and experiences. Ryan's perspective and analysis of crucial skills are broken down and explained brilliantly. His conversational tone and thoughtful analogies make this book a fantastic resource for presenters.

Rachelle Iafrate, Chief of Staff, CBI Health Group

The Effective Presenter

The Winning Formula for Business Presentations

The Effective Presenter

The Winning Formula for Business Presentations

Ryan J. Warriner

BUSINESS
BOOKS

Winchester, UK
Washington, USA

JOHN HUNT PUBLISHING

First published by Business Books, 2022
Business Books is an imprint of John Hunt Publishing Ltd., No. 3 East St., Alresford,
Hampshire SO24 9EE, UK
office@jhpbooks.com
www.johnhuntpublishing.com
www.johnhuntpublishing.com/business-books

For distributor details and how to order please visit the 'Ordering' section on our website.

ISBN: 978 1 78904 795 0
978 1 78904 796 7 (ebook)
Library of Congress Control Number: 2020947598

A CIP catalogue record for this book is available from the British Library.

Design: Stuart Davies

UK: Printed and bound by CPI Group (UK) Ltd, Croydon, CR0 4YY
Printed in North America by CPI GPS partners

We operate a distinctive and ethical publishing philosophy in
all areas of our business, from our global network of authors to
production and worldwide distribution.

Contents

This book is dedicated to my friends in the business sector. May this book be a resource for you in all of your future endeavours.

"To do more for the world than the world does for you, that is success."

Henry Ford

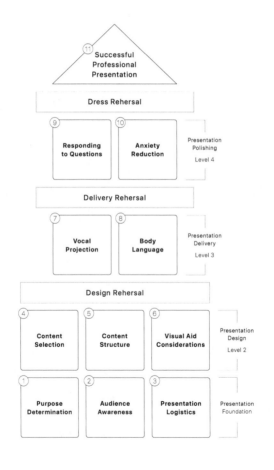

Preface

Impetus

You have an upcoming, professional presentation. You're thinking about when you'll start working on it and what it should include. You're pondering the positive and negative consequences of your presentation. As you get started, you begin second guessing yourself. You feel like you're missing something or you're not sure if you'll meet expectations. You review your content repeatedly hoping to find something to improve, but are unable to squash that constant feeling of unease. Time's running out, and you realize that you'll have to present what you have—and hope that it's acceptable. Sound familiar? You're not alone. This is the process that many professionals endure each time they are tasked with delivering a presentation. This guide has been designed specifically to address these concerns and help professionals, like you, succeed.

What's the best feeling for a presenter to have before, during, and after their professional presentation? The answer is *peace of mind*: the comfort of knowing that you've checked-off all of the boxes and set yourself up for success!

What That Feels Like...

Imagine yourself about to step in front of an audience. Instead of second guessing yourself and hoping that you've included everything pertinent or that others will be pleased with your presentation, you're calm and confident knowing that you've considered all aspects of your presentation and not left anything to chance. It's like the feeling of submitting a valuable project or proposal that has met every criterion, knowing that you've nailed the expectation, versus the feeling of crossing your fingers and simply hoping for the best. In essence, this guide provides the comfort of knowing that you included everything valuable, in the optimal structure customized for your content, and the confidence to address any outstanding concerns.

This guide will strengthen your overall speaking confidence and provide you with all of the tools, tips, and approaches required to be successful.

You don't need to be an industry-leading expert, or a captivating, energetic speaker, to be a highly effective presenter. Presenting successfully is not a gift. No one is born a great presenter. Presenting is like a muscle: the more you work it, the more it develops, and the stronger it becomes.

The Professional Presentation Framework

This book centers on a proven presentation framework and outlines the complete formula to help you prepare, design, and deliver an

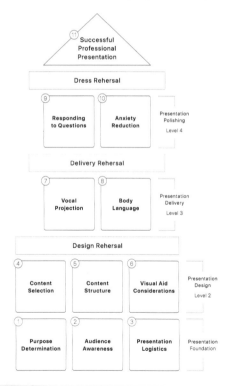

effective presentation. Following this framework will ensure that you, the presenter, are ready to facilitate a meaningful, impactful, and memorable presentation. You'll have afforded yourself the highest probability of success.

In this guide, the steps to producing a successful, professional presentation have been organized systematically into four levels:

1. Foundation
2. Design
3. Delivery
4. Polish

Of course, there will be times when these levels overlap and inform one another. Ultimately, all of the components factor into a single, comprehensive equation. To best utilize and implement this proven framework consider the following guidelines:

1. The more accurate information you have regarding each *Foundation* component, the more likely your presentation will be a success.
2. The individual components of a professional presentation influence each other. When presenters overlook a step or two, there is a ripple effect that causes other components to be less accurate. (Think of it like an ecosystem: if you remove one animal or organism from its environment, all other organisms will be affected to some degree.)
3. This book is designed to be utilized sequentially as a holistic process, but has been compartmentalized into specific, manageable sections for those of you looking to refine your skills in a particular area.

Follow the Framework

This book is supplemented with many, relevant experiences of soft-spoken introverts producing successful presentations regularly because they have understood and followed its framework. If you're willing to trust yourself and your ability to learn, you'll be surprised and impressed by the level of growth in your confidence and presentation skills.

This guide focuses on universal presentation skill development that is applicable to a wide array of contexts. It is far more advantageous to understand and develop essential presentation skills, and then customize your presentation to your circumstances through the framework. In short, this guide provides overarching principles and approaches that can enhance your presentation skills in any workplace.

Presentation Navigation

As you read, you'll find that the recipe to produce and perform a successful, professional presentation has been laid out in a specific sequence. The knowledge and skills in this guide are unpacked methodically in a way that shows you how to avoid common, potential pitfalls and guarantees improving your success-rate time and time again.

Introduction

Understanding Professional Presentations

A presentation is a structured form of oral communication designed to achieve a specific outcome. In most cases, it involves one person (the presenter) speaking to multiple people (the audience). On the surface, most presentations involve a combination of speaking and body language (stage presence), and many also call for visual aids to supplement the spoken content. However, just like a Hollywood blockbuster, there's much more that goes into the development, than the final product seen by audiences. For the purposes of this guide, the definitions and understandings of professional presentations are outlined below.

Effective Vs. Ineffective

Not all presentations are created equal. Some presentations are clearly more effective and impactful than others. I'm sure that, at some point, you've had the displeasure of sitting through a presentation, thinking to yourself: "Why am I here?", "What are they talking about?", or "We already know this!" Typically, during these dry presentations, members of the audience are left to daydream, chit-chat, or check their phones. There are also overloaded presentations, which may cause the audience to think: "You lost me about ten minutes ago." This concept is like loading thousands of pounds of cargo into a van, and then being surprised when the van won't move. Each of these scenarios is not the fault of the audience. The negative outcomes are a direct result of poor preparation, design, and/or delivery in the professional presentation process.

Conversely, you may have observed a presentation that made you think: "Good, this makes sense!" or, "Perfect! Now I know what to do." These presentations inspire engagement and interest from the audience. Obviously, we would all aim for the latter in these examples, but how do we get there? What are the differences between these presentations, and what makes one superior to the other? Many of us can determine the effectiveness of a presentation as an audience member, but then struggle to replicate that effectiveness in our own presentations. Through this guide, you will find clear markers and a fully developed framework to help you design and deliver an effective professional presentation that you would want to listen to.

Professional Presentation Vs. Public Speaking

Nowadays, many people confuse public speaking with professional presentations. To set the record straight, there are many types of public speaking, with the professional presentation being one of those types. Consider the visual below:

Public Speaking

TED talks and Toast Masters are excellent examples of public speaking, but not necessarily of professional presentations. What's the difference? It starts with the purpose of each. Public speaking typically has a more general purpose. Most often, it's to raise awareness about a particular issue or share a different perspective. It could also be to inspire, motivate, or entertain. In fact, TED is an acronym that represents *Technology Entertainment Design*. The key word being "entertainment." Another example to consider is a comedian's act. Stand-up comedy is a form of public speaking, but we wouldn't consider a comedian on stage to be a professional presenter.

With a more general purpose and widely applicable message, a public speaker's audience is typically more diverse. For example, there is a video circulating on the internet of a TED talk exploring the Marshmallow Challenge. The speaker, Tom Wujec from Autodesk, had collected data on different teams of people as they attempted to build the tallest structure with specific and limited supplies. The main message of the video was that "teamwork and belonging" are stronger contributors to group success than level of intellect. This emphasis on teamwork and belonging can be widely applied to different situations and is not limited to a single, actionable scenario.

Professional Presentations

In a professional presentation, the desired outcome is more focused, the audience is more specific, and the venue is often more exclusive. The desired outcome is not to entertain nor to captivate the audience, but to bring a specific result to fruition (i.e., investment, sale, update, etc.). The audience consists of people who are directly and significantly impacted by the presentation's content. The atmosphere is professional, focused, and driven by results.

Success is measured by the degree to which presenters have achieved their desired outcome(s). Both presentation goals and desired outcomes will be expanded upon in Chapter One, *Specifying Purpose*, but it is worth noting that this guide uses them as both the target, and the measuring stick, of success.

Comparison

The difference between public speaking and professional presentations is similar to the difference between a general medical practitioner and a medical specialist, with a key distinction being the audience. Public speaking and TED talks attract audiences from all walks of life on a variety of different topics. Because their range in audience is so vast, speakers must create an entertaining speech with widely relevant data. This is like a family doctor giving health advice to the masses such as: take vitamins, sleep sufficiently, and exercise regularly, which is quite useful and widely applicable. But such advice is not to be confused with that of a cardiologist, who can prescribe treatment after a double bypass operation. This is what a professional presentation is: a focused, specific oral communication, for a specific audience, to bring about a targeted outcome.

Being a Professional

This guide foregrounds professional presentations, which are, quite simply, presentations that take place in the professional sector. In the first chapter you'll learn the relationship between presentation goals and desired outcome(s). One of your presentation goals that you'll establish as you progress through the framework will be to project yourself as prepared, composed, well-spoken, and professional. This aspect also includes being well-dressed and groomed, arriving early, and being respectful to the audience. Ultimately, you need to look objectively at yourself as a presenter and ask yourself: "Would I choose me to be an ambassador for my company, organization, or department?" By this standard, being charismatic or charming is not as valuable as being professional.

A Shift in Perspective

A professional presentation is not ONE VS. MANY. It is not YOU VS.

AUDIENCE. It is YOU + AUDIENCE VS. YOUR COMPETITORS/PAST PERFORMANCE/THE FUTURE/ UNCHARTED TERRITORY. We will explore this perspective more thoroughly later on in this guide. It is key to strengthening confidence, as well as designing and producing more effective, professional presentations. Adopting this perspective is the first step in improving your skill set.

The ancient philosophy called "stoicism" provides the most accurate and realistic lens through which to view professional presentations. To give you an idea of stoic methodology, let's consider archery. A stoic would say: imagine that you have an upcoming archery competition in two months time. You begin practicing shooting a bow and arrow hundreds of times per day to improve your accuracy. You acquire the best equipment and partake in the best training each day. When the competition day comes, you take your mark, and line yourself up as best as possible. You are completely prepared and have done everything in your power to achieve success. You release your arrow. At this exact point, the result is out of your control. The wind may suddenly pick up and blow your arrow off-course, or perhaps the target may have moved. Some elements are out of your control. They should be acknowledged, but not focused upon. A stoic would feel proud and content with their efforts knowing that they've done everything in their power to move the needle in their favor.

Professional presentations should be approached as the stoics' view archery. Your focus should be on preparing yourself to perform effectively. Your goal should not be to receive a standing ovation or a pat on the back for your presentation, but to bring a specific outcome to fruition. The professional presentation framework has been strategically designed to achieve a specific outcome. Chapter One (*Specifying Purpose*) focuses on desired outcomes, but for now, understand that the common misconceptions (e.g., being entertaining, being charming, being charismatic, etc.) which some believe to be integral to an effective professional presentation, are exactly that: misconceptions.

Trust the Process

The framework is the result of science, research, practice, and experience combined. Following this framework will ensure that you have not omitted any valuable components of your presentation and that you have undoubtedly set yourself up for success. To become most effective and stand out from your colleagues and competitors, trust the process. Complete each step as fully and accurately as

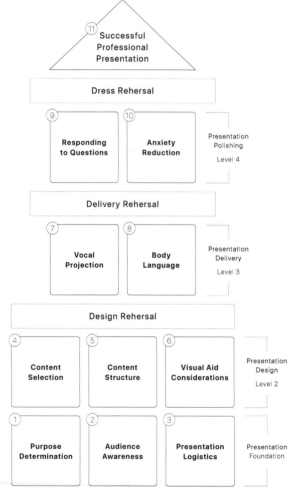

possible given your situation. If you focus on the framework, your desired results will come organically. You should approach your professional presentations with this mindset and understanding. Imagine there are two people going to the gym to exercise every day. One person focuses all of their attention on performing their exercises properly. The second person focuses on simply completing their workout and leaving the gym. Who do you think will achieve superior results?

"The will to prepare to win is greater than the will to win."
– Vince Lombardi

Value of a Professional Presentation

Delivering a presentation is often viewed as an unpleasant experience that most people would be happy to avoid. Think back to grade school when the teacher asked a question and students stared at their desks, attempting to avoid sharing their response in front of their classmates. Many people, in fact, have reported that their greatest fear in life—even above the fear of death—is speaking in front of an audience. Comedian Jerry Seinfeld, once made the joke that if a person had to be involved in a funeral, they would prefer to be in the casket, rather than delivering the eulogy.

Power of Oral Communication

Clearly, there's compelling evidence that professional presentations can be a nerve-racking experience for the everyday industry professional turned presenter. And we know from our experience as audience members that presentations can lack value, or be so overloaded with content that nothing gets absorbed. So why are presentations still being requested and delivered? Why not simply send the necessary information in a report or memo to the relevant parties? Why are we placed in the position to stand up in front of others and orally communicate our content? The answer is because of the notion that content can be more effectively delivered and absorbed, orally.

Most humans learn to listen before reading.[1] There is overwhelming evidence that listening is humanity's most frequent vessel of communication. In an average day, people listen about three times more than they read.[2] People are more receptive, have longer attention spans, and are more likely to retain content when listening as opposed to reading. Consider human history: people have been communicating through reading and writing for approximately 5500 years.[3,4] On the other hand, people have communicated through speaking, listening, and interpreting body language since the beginning of communication, more than 100 000 years ago.[5] At the end of the day, most people are far more adept at communicating orally than via text.

Guided Reception

There are two supplementary benefits of a professional presentation. The first is the ability to connect with the audience. This affords the presenter the opportunity to switch tactics or adapt to audience members. Years ago, as a college professor, I was assessing an intern while they presented their company's options regarding product procurement. The products were organized by their cost and their value. When the presenter began by stating the price of the first product, the audience nodded along. However, when the presenter moved on to the value that the product would bring, the audience stopped nodding. While the presenter was explaining how they came to that value, each audience member tilted their head. I could almost hear a collective "huh?" of confusion.

At this point, the presenter had lost the audience. It was at this critical juncture when the intern's presentation was at a make-or-break point. If the presenter had been able to read the audience accurately, they would have determined that many people were confused or had stopped following the presentation. The presenter could have recovered by interjecting and stating: "Alright, let me go back through the value for this product" or "Ok, I'm sensing that we've disconnected somewhere. Let me try to explain that another way," then explained again how the product would bring value in greater, more accessible detail. The presentation would have been more likely to succeed. The audience would have felt more involved and understood, and the presenter would have felt more confident knowing that they had connected with their audience. However, the presenter chose to simply disregard the audience's puzzled facial expressions and, instead, soldier on through their presentation. As a result, the audience immediately became disengaged and less attentive. The presenter signaled their lack of regard for the audience, and the audience responded accordingly.

Enhanced Engagement

A professional presentation can also be interactive. Typically, the smaller the audience size, the more interactive it will be. Nevertheless, because the presenter is physically in front of the audience, sharing information, the audience is able to engage more with the presentation. Consider the difference between speaking with a human service representative on the phone, versus a company automated service. Most of us prefer to speak with an actual person on the other end of the line.

Many of the questions that presenters are asked are either clarification questions or expansion questions (refer to Chapter Nine, *Responding to Questions*). This, in turn, allows for more comprehensive understanding and it also ensures that all parties in attendance are apprised of the content. This is a significant advantage for many managers and executives who aim to ensure that all of their colleagues are made aware of a pertinent issue, such as a revised company policy, for example.

Cloaked Opportunity

On one occasion, I was approached to consult with, and then coach, a junior manager for a fortune 500 company. This junior manager, let's call him Jim, was summoned by his director to present the financial forecasting data that he had been working on. Jim immediately panicked. He felt his presenting skills were a little rusty and his director had never asked anything of him directly before. In fact, he had very little contact with the director of his department. The first and dominant thought in his mind was: "If I mess this up, I'll be passed-over, demoted, or even fired. Maybe they'll restructure and I'll be considered redundant." Shortly thereafter, Jim was referred to me by a colleague. After a brief conversation wherein he expressed his concern, I told him that I was uncertain as to what would happen in the aftermath of his presentation. I explained that I didn't have a crystal ball. But I also assured him of what we could do. Which was to prepare, design, and rehearse the delivery of the presentation to maximize his probability of success. Thinking back to the stoicism example of releasing the arrow, we, as presenters, can only influence so much. After a certain point, our fate is out of our hands. Jim agreed and we collaborated on his presentation. The result was positive— with a surprise twist.

Jim contacted me a few hours after his presentation and told me it went well. He said that he felt good, that he felt the presentation was clear, and that he had addressed all of the audience members' questions (which was one of his biggest worries). A few days later, he called me again to let me know that he had just been promoted to senior manager, and was going to be given a larger office and team to help him going forward. I felt tremendously happy for him. His presentation had worked out better than initially expected. He was able to compose himself and focus on producing an effective, meaningful presentation. About a month later, he sent me an email. He said that he had gotten to know his director much better in his new role and had uncovered that he was being considered for a promotion before he was asked to present. All of the potential negative consequences that were in his mind prior to presenting were pure fiction. The moral of the story is that presentations are opportunities, not tests, and should be approached as such.

Chapter One

Specifying Purpose

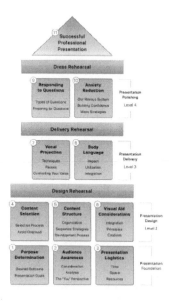

Desired Outcomes and Goal Establishment

When you're faced with an upcoming professional presentation, the *purpose* is the most important component and it must be identified. Without identifying one, you risk producing a rambling, unfocused presentation that is likely to result in a waste of time and resources. It's like having to drive to a work retreat and not identifying the location in advance. Your *ad hoc* plan is essentially: "Well, I'll just get started in what I think is the right direction, and hope I arrive there on time—if at all." Most of us would never do this in real life, yet it's an unfortunately common approach that many presenters take. Instead, I offer an alternative that will help you hone in on what you hope to achieve and, through the process outlined below, increase your likelihood of achieving it.

Purpose Determination Process

1. Specify your desired outcome
2. Determine criteria (goals) that would help to bring your desired outcome to fruition
3. Progress through the framework with your goals in mind
4. Continually refine and determine how you can accomplish your goals

Desired Outcome

Think of your *purpose* as the *desired outcome(s)* that you would like to transpire as a result of your presentation. In other words, avoid thinking of the purpose as: "Why am I here?" Instead, think: "What do I want to happen as a result of my presentation?" This is your desired outcome. Most of the time, the desired outcome involves your audience. For example, in an investment pitch to venture capitalists, your desired outcome might be to secure a particular amount of investment for your company. Here, your desired outcome is in the form of an action that your audience must take. Once you have concluded your presentation, its potential implications are out of your hands. However, what's in your hands is your preparation leading up to that particular moment. Your presentation goals, on the other hand, are criteria that you set for yourself to be successful. These are more easily measured and increase the probability of achieving your desired outcome.

In the example, your goals may be to emphasize your most promising opportunity, present your value or benefits in a logical sequence, and present yourself in a respectful, professional manner. Successful presentations focus on only one or two desired outcomes, but multiple goals. The more goals that you accomplish throughout the course of your presentation, the more likely you are to bring your desired outcome to fruition. And that's the truest measurement of success.

Visit www.professionalpresentationservices.com to access the free supplementary resources

Establishing your Goals

As you work your way through this guide, you will begin to establish your presentation goals. They consist of tangible actions that you can take to improve your chances of achieving your desired outcome. Determining your goals may take some time. In this part of the process, you should consider what the potential best-case scenario is for you, and then work your way backwards.

Once you have established your desired outcome (at the beginning of the professional presentation process), brainstorm what you can do and/or what to include during your presentation to increase the probability of it. You shouldn't spend too much time on establishing your goals at the beginning of your presentation. It's good to have a general idea of what they could be, but you'll find that your goals will become firmed up and refined as you progress through the framework. By the time the curtain goes up on presentation day, you will have established clear goals for success. The more specific you can make your goals, the better. When you specify your goals in the form of tangible, checklist criteria, you are more likely to design and deliver effectively. Ending up with vague goals such as "present effectively" or "be clear" will be difficult to measure and leave you less focused on accomplishing them.

Side Note: In my experience consulting and collaborating with industry professionals, establishing presentation goals and desired outcomes can be the most challenging step in the process. They are also the most integral part of the process, so don't get discouraged. Stay focused and work your way back from the best-case scenario. Think: what would need to happen to get there?

Understand your Focus

Don't confuse inspiring orators with effective presenters. Your aim should be to accomplish specific presentation goals that contribute to achieving your desired outcome. Your speaking skills will develop, your body language will improve, and your confidence will increase, as long as you focus on establishing and achieving your presentation goals. Being charismatic, enthusiastic, and articulate are not requirements to become a highly effective presenter. Your next professional presentation should be approached with this understanding in mind.

Your desired outcome is achieved indirectly, but your goals are achieved directly. This is a crucial component of crafting a professional presentation, yet it is constantly overlooked. Let's expand on the earlier example of a presentation aimed at increasing sales revenue via purchase orders. The final, specified desired outcome would be to increase purchase orders by persuading the audience that the product or service is superior to the competition. Now, you can focus more easily on establishing your presentation goals. What content will most likely be meaningful to our audience? Understanding your audience is a key factor in the goal establishment process, but we will explore this point more in Chapter Two. What sequence or organization of content would be easiest for them to follow? What is their past experience with the product or service? The answers to these questions will begin to shape our presentation goals. With every slide that we create, and every line that we rehearse, we ask ourselves: "Does this support or illustrate my product/service as superior?" This approach will unify our presentation, improving its clarity, effectiveness, and probability of success. Not to mention the time it will save in preparing.

Determining Success

One of my fondest presentation memories was when I was consulting with a growing start-up company that was seeking investment. I was collaborating with the founder and CEO to optimize their presentation to investors. I asked him what he wanted the outcome to be. He told me that he had always been shaky in professional presentations and, as a result, he'd really like to present more smoothly.

As we spoke more, he stated that, overall, he wanted to appear polished and likeable to his audience. So, I asked him, "If, at the end of your presentation, your audience views you as polished and approachable, you'd consider that a success?"

He paused, and tilted his head in thought. "Well," he explained, "We also need to obtain investment capital."

I smiled and began to gesture with my hands while saying, "We need to flip those around. Acquiring a target amount of investment capital is your desired outcome. Being polished and likeable may help us get there." Again, he paused, contemplating what I had just said.

Then I asked, "How much investment are we aiming for?"

He replied, "7.5 million is the target, but if we raise more than 6.5, I'll be happy."

From there, we set out to give our arrow the best chance of hitting that "bullseye."

Together, we established quantifiable goals that would help us to persuade the venture capitalists to invest. None were to get the audience to like him. I spent hours designing, coaching, and rehearsing with him leading up until the big day. Unfortunately, I was scheduled to lead a workshop on the day of his presentation, so I was unable to observe him first hand. But he promised to keep me posted on the outcome. I received an email from him a few days later.

It read: "Sorry I've been out of touch. Presentation went really well. We're actually still securing investment funding!"

I replied, "That's Great! Did we hit the target?"

He responded, "Better! We got over 10!"

Not a word about "being liked".

Communication Breakdown

The ancient Roman orator and philosopher, Cicero, determined that we communicate for three distinct purposes. The three being to inform, to persuade, or to entertain. When it comes to professional presentations, the purpose will never be to entertain. You may choose to incorporate entertaining tactics such as humor, to increase the reception of your presentation, but it should not be the focus of the presentation. The primary, desired outcome of your presentation will boil down to either informing or persuading the audience.

Nearly every time that I speak on this topic, I ask the question: "How will you measure the success of your presentation?" And nearly every time I get the same two responses. Most people respond saying, "by including everything important," meaning that if they've presented everything that they've prepared, and haven't omitted anything, it's a success. Unfortunately, not leaving anything out doesn't ensure that you've chosen the right content to present, or that your audience was receptive. If your audience isn't receptive, you've already failed. Others have remarked that if the audience has remembered or retained the presentation content afterwards, it is a success. While being memorable does indicate that your audience was receptive on some level, it still doesn't confirm that you've presented the best content, or that you have presented it in an effective way. I have easily observed and analyzed more than a thousand presentations throughout my career, of all different sorts. I can tell you quite confidently that some of the most vivid memories I have are of the presentations that have either misfired or failed.

The central purpose of a professional presentation is either to bring your audience up to speed on a specific topic (to inform), or to influence your audience to do or believe something (to persuade). Gauge the success of your next presentation accordingly. If your purpose is to inform or raise your audience's awareness, you should assess how much more educated or informed they are as a result of your presentation. Of course, I'm not suggesting that you should test them on your presentation's content. But ask yourself: "Did I provide them with enough adequate information to make an informed decision or to proceed in their respective roles?" Ultimately, this will be measured over time, when people either proceed with their new understanding, or they begin to ask questions that had been previously addressed in your presentation. Or they might not change their behaviors at all. If your purpose is to persuade the audience to purchase your product or service, you should assess how many more purchase orders you have as a result of your presentation.

Winning Analogy

You can think about the relationship between your presentation goals and desired outcome like an American football game. A football team's desired outcome for their upcoming matchup is to win the game. However, when they are practicing, preparing, and strategizing, they do not focus on winning the game. Instead, they focus on a handful of key criteria (goals), such as limiting their team's turnovers, controlling possession of the football, and eliminating explosive plays by the opposition. If they accomplish these goals, it does not guarantee that they will win the game, but it will increase the probability that they do.

Success in the Real World

I was once collaborating on a presentation with the CTO of a growing tech company in the southern U.S. The company's flagship product was a web-based platform which its clients used to better serve their customers in the business to business (B2B) realm. He was presenting to a large group of clients on some of the new features that his company had built into the platform. While he explained his situation to me, the conversation went something like this:

Me: Okay, what is your desired outcome? What would be the best-case scenario as a result of your presentation? And what are your goals?

CTO: Well… I guess it would be to have our clients understand the new features that we've added.

Me: Understand what they are/do? Or understand how to use them efficiently?

CTO: Both.

Me: Okay, so why is it important for them to understand this information?

CTO: Well, because we'd like them to use the features and test out the new functionality.

Me: What will that do for you?

CTO: They might use it in a manner that we haven't anticipated and we depend on their feedback to improve and refine our platform.

Me: Okay! Now we're getting there! So, your desired outcome is for your clients to use the new features and provide you with ample, meaningful feedback. Your presentation goals are roughly to explain the functionality of the features, showcase the benefits of the new features, express that their priorities are important to you, and explain connections between their feedback and product evolution. But these goals will get more refined as we get closer to your presentation.

CTO: Oh, I like that! That is exactly what I'd like to happen.

Me: Perfect. Let's make it happen!

One factor to keep in mind is the difference between influence and control. You will have some influence in your professional presentation, but understand and accept that some factors are simply out of our control. Think back on our stoic approach to archery; your desired outcome is to hit the bullseye. You prepare and practice to hit the bullseye, but remember that once you release the arrow, the outcome is out of your control. You only have influence on the outcome until the arrow leaves your fingertips. Think of achieving the desired outcome of your presentation in this way.

Regardless of the results of your presentation, one notion will be certain to all parties concerned: you are a prepared professional who can be trusted to produce when called upon. And that is an invaluable element of your reputation.

Chapter Two

Interpreting Your Audience

Understanding your audience is crucial to maximizing your presentation's effectiveness. Your audience is your counterpart in the presentation and their importance cannot be overstated. In fact, your desired outcome may be impossible to achieve without knowledge of your audience. Imagine yourself as the GPS guiding system on a journey, and your audience is driving the vehicle. The purpose or desired outcome is your destination. Knowing your audience is like identifying the starting point, best route to take, and optimal speed to travel. The more familiar you are with your audience, the better you can plan your route (design your presentation), the more accurately you can guide them (accomplish presentation goals), and the more likely they are to arrive at your destination (achieve your desired outcome).

The Four Key Audience Considerations

1. Audience Empathy
2. Audience Values and Priorities
3. Audience Thought Process
4. Audience Current Knowledge Base

Determining these key audience considerations will increase your professional presentation's success. It's not impossible to execute an effective presentation without fully understanding your audience, but it is extremely difficult. Think of it as designing a suit or dress for someone. The more information that you have about your client, the more you can tailor your fabric to meet their needs and wants, which in turn, increases the probability of your product's success. To get you started, I've created a process called the "Audience Analysis" to provide you with critical insight.

1. Audience Empathy

The first part of analyzing the audience is to put yourself in the shoes of your audience members. In the private sector, the majority of executives have hundreds of tasks to address or accomplish in a given day. So, their time is at a premium. Yet, they will be sitting in front of you for a period of their day. They are doing so with the assumption that you will provide value to them. Perhaps you will be saving them time or money, or you'll be sharing essential information for them to take the next step in their respective projects.

Whatever their reason for attending is, the presumption is that you will be adding value to them in their role. The question becomes: how will *you* help *them*? From the audiences' perspective, "Why do I need to know this?" This question can often be confused with your presentation's purpose, but it can differ from your desired outcome (refer to Chapter One, *Specifying Purpose*). Before you begin to design your presentation, you must first obtain a strong understanding of why your audience plans to attend and how you can help them. Think about what your audience will be able to do, or be inclined to do, as a result of attending your presentation, that they might not have before.

Audience Empathy Guiding Questions

- Why are you presenting to them in the first place?
- How are you going to help them?
- How will they benefit from your presentation?
- What can you do for them?
- Why do they need to know this information?

The One-Size-Fits-All Trap

On another occasion, I was invited to help solve a problem that a team of executives was having within their respective organization. The issue was explained to me at length. The basis of it was that an individual within the company was routinely being tasked with delivering professional presentations, but was producing a wide range of inconsistent results. Sometimes, he hit the bullseye (achieving his desired outcome), but sometimes he misfired in the entirely opposite direction, and everything in between. So, I began to investigate and run a diagnostic assessment. I asked a few strategic, systematic questions to some of the key players in the scenario. After a short time, I discovered a handful of commonalities and a major part of the problem. The executive was typically required to present on the same topic for three different audiences in a short period of time. First, the executive was to prepare and present the nature of organizational policy changes to the board of directors. Next, they were to inform their employees of these changes, in the form of a presentation. Finally, they were to update their product distributors in a larger presentation.

The executive began by creating one presentation for their board of directors, which focused on the positive impact of work flow as well as big picture benefits to the company. The executive then continued to use the same presentation, down to the visual aids, with the next two, very different audiences. Basically, the executive used the same presentation for three different audiences and, as a result, the presentations decreased in effectiveness each time. Product distributors are more concerned with how the new changes impact them and their role. In reality, they hope that the company they distribute for does well, but sharing the same content that the board received is practically meaningless for them.

I recall the executive being very upset and disappointed when they had realized their error. What's more is that their interpretation of my diagnosis was that they needed to invest more of their already limited time to customizing multiple variations of the presentation. I explained to them that I was glad because this fix would be very easy. I went on to explain that we would need to tweak and frame the content differently for each audience. We started by determining what we wanted to occur as a result of each presentation (desired outcome). We practiced putting ourselves in the shoes of our audience members and asking ourselves: "If I were them, how would this policy change impact my role?" Because the audience is different in each presentation, the desired outcome changes accordingly; which, in turn, leads to changes in presentation content, design, and delivery.

Here's a snapshot of what we ended up with:

Board of Directors
- Big picture focus: how the changes in policy will impact the organization as a whole.

Employees
- More micro focus: workflow changes and the new project development operational procedure.

Product Distributors
- How and when they will receive the shipments of products to distribute.
- How to track and catalogue their product distribution.

Each audience has a different perspective, set of values, and interests. Consequently, each requires a uniquely tailored presentation that speaks to their roles and needs. This concept leads to the process of content selection, which is outlined in Chapter Four (*Content Selection*), but for now keep in mind that each new audience calls for a separate presentation. For the executive, this was an eye-opening experience and has paid dividends ever since.

2. Audience Values and Priorities

The next part of your audience analysis focuses on their values and points of interest. In the business world, many executives prioritize profits and losses. Therefore, sometimes, it's as simple as maximizing profits, or minimizing losses. Other times, it's making a process more efficient, or increasing health and safety awareness. Wherever their values lie, it's important for the presenter to accurately identify them, and demonstrate an understanding of them. Understanding an audience's values will help you to focus your presentation on the information that is most meaningful for them, which will increase your effectiveness. In doing so, you're demonstrating an understanding of, and appreciation for, their values. This shows them that you recognize their individual interests and needs. Your stock will rise in turn.

Audience Values and Priorities Guiding Questions

- What do they value most?
- What is their priority?
- What is important for them to consider in their role?

3. Audience Thought Process

The next audience insight that you should pursue is the type of evidence or information that will most resonate with members attending your presentation. Does your audience prefer more qualitative or quantitative information—or both? This knowledge and understanding of your audience will help you to achieve the above point which is: how you can best help or influence them. Think about how your audience interprets information and what will be most useful for them. Remember that their life goes on after your presentation, so what type of information can you present to them, and in what order, to improve their efficiency or effectiveness? What message do you want the audience to take away with them? For example, I once observed a presentation facilitated by an up-and-coming, international production company. The speakers spent the majority of their presentation explaining how new production and manufacturing facilities in three new countries would benefit the company. They went on at length to explain the multitude of benefits that their company would enjoy. Unfortunately, their audience members were more concerned with the logistics and respective international bureaucracy that would come with each new facility. This presentation was not well received, as a result of *audience assumption* or miscalculation.

Audience's Thought Process Guiding Questions

- What type of evidence will convince them that you're correct?
- What type of data are they accustomed to seeing?
- Do they prefer headlines only, or are they more detail-oriented?
- Which data or information is most valuable for them to have?
- What type of evidence will help them to make a decision?

4. Audience Current Knowledge Base

The last audience consideration that you should endeavour to determine is how much your audience knows about your presentation topic already. What knowledge are they going in with? This detail will help you to find the "sweet spot" of both language and content. The goal is to avoid going into too much detail and using topic-specific terminology (jargon) that they won't understand. Avoid being redundant; do not waste their time with information that they already know. Being able to accurately gauge your audience's knowledge base on the topic of your presentation will help you scaffold to them. Meaning that you'll be effectively able to build a bridge between what they already know and what you want them to know (presentation goals). Then you'll be able to guide them over that bridge through your presentation.

Audience's Current Knowledge Base Guiding Questions

- How much does my audience already know about the content

of my presentation?

- How much of the language that I plan to use are they familiar with?

One of my first clients was an educational technology company based in Canada. Being that I had experience in the education sector, I was invited to lend my expertise in showcasing their latest product favorably, and also to share my insights on the market itself. Their strategy was to hire former teachers and retired educational administrators. The idea was to leverage their contacts and connections and sell the company's products. However, the problem was that these educators-turned-sales-reps were not trained in sales and had little knowledge of professional presentations. I came to realize that the reason I had been contacted in the first place was due to their lack of sales. Fortunately for me, the issue at hand was one that I was prepared to resolve. These former educators were not preparing professional presentations for their contacts and prospective buyers but, rather, teaching them about the product.

I had accompanied a few of them to their scheduled presentations. To my astonishment, they were explaining how the products work as if the audience members were children. They were speaking excessively slowly, nodding, and saying "okay" every other word with drawn-out, rising intonation. They were constantly confirming that the audience was following along. Red flags were going up in my mind as I was attempting to put my finger on the core issue. After reflecting on the events, I realized that they had a comprehensive understanding of the product, but approached the audience as if they were young students. It seemed as though they had defaulted back to "school teaching mode" when they stepped on stage. You can imagine how I felt providing their superior with my review and take on what happened. But that was indeed the case. When we followed up with a few of the audience members, they reported terms like "awkward" and "uncomfortable," which I interpreted as the polite way of saying "insulting" or "condescending." In the end, ensure that your presentation matches your audience's level of content understanding and you will have assured yourself stronger reception.

Performing an Audience Analysis

Oftentimes, you will know the majority of your audience, but on the occasion that you don't, it's a good idea to approach this situation with discretion. An audience analysis consists of addressing the four key audience considerations outlined earlier. The first step in the process is to put yourself in your audience member's shoes. Then work your way through the four considerations. It's useful to reflect on your audience member's past behavior as you begin to hone your understanding of them. After you've exhausted your own knowledge base on your audience, consider external sources. A colleague or event coordinator are possible assets in this situation. But you must approach this situation tactfully. The question that I get most often is: What am I supposed to say? The answer is to state your hypothesis, then request confirmation, as opposed to asking a direct question. For example, you might ask a colleague, "The people attending my presentation next Thursday will be representatives from our financial department, correct?" as opposed to "Who can I expect my audience to be?" or "Who'll be there?" The latter may indicate that you've missed a detail that was explained earlier, while the former indicates foresight and initiative. In return, your colleague will be much more inclined to provide you with accurate follow-up information. Experience has demonstrated that this strategy has a proven track record.

The four key audience considerations of the "Audience Analysis" have been carefully created to maximize effectiveness and minimize time spent on presentation development. Your time is valuable, so don't get bogged down with "average age" or anything more micro. They are far less important than the considerations above. Once you've completed the audience analysis, you're set to proceed through the framework with confidence.

When envisioning your audience, focus on one person in the audience. Regardless of whether your audience is three people or 3000 people, design it with one typical person in mind. This process will help you to focus on their specific values and perspectives, which will translate to the majority, as opposed to attempting to consider all who might be present.

Another useful strategy is to send out a memo or pre-presentation info sheet/document that outlines some key prior content that your audience should be aware of heading into the presentation. This is most utilized during internal presentations. It doesn't have to be long or complicated; it can be bulleted or visual-based. The goal is to bring your audience members up to speed in a professional and engaging way.

Visit www.professionalpresentationservices.com to access the free supplementary resources

Presentation Grounding

Keeping your audience in mind along with your desired outcome is integral throughout the entirety of your professional presentation process. The content that you choose to include, the sequence that you choose to unpack the content in, and the visual aids that you choose to complement your presentation all play a role.

Everything should be prepared and designed with your audience and desired outcome firmly in mind.

Once you have narrowed down both, consider writing them down so that you can refer to them throughout the professional presentation framework. This technique is called "presentation grounding" because it will keep you from wandering down avenues that are not essential, wasting your precious time, and increasing the risk of misfiring on your presentation.

All Things to All People

A few years back, I was collaborating with a building manager and reviewing a presentation that he had created for the supervisors working within the building. The idea was that they would then convey the key concepts to their respective employees and other professionals who worked onsite. He indicated to me that the reason he requested my services was because his last presentation was not very well understood by the supervisors, and he had to answer so many follow-up questions that took longer to address than the presentation itself. He wanted to avoid that this time around.

As we reviewed his former presentation, one visual aid stood out to me immediately and I quickly zeroed in on it. It was a fire evacuation plan for the premises that he oversaw. It looked so complicated and cluttered. Each of the 14 floors were outlined in the same diagram— complete with directional arrows, landmarks, fire extinguisher locations, and different colours to indicate anticipated traffic!

I stopped him at this slide and asked, "What is this visual for?"

"To show how to evacuate in case of a fire," he responded.

I thought to myself, "We need to come at this from another angle." I said, "Okay, who made this visual aid? And for what purpose?"

He replied: "Oh, well, originally myself and the fire inspector hashed it out one day so that the building was up to code."

"That's it. That's the reason," I said while nodding.

I went on to explain that this visual was perfect for the fire inspector to approve the building as operational, but it didn't yield much value for its inhabitants.

I informed him that each of the supervisors that he would be presenting to (his audience), would need to understand how their employees and professionals are expected to safely exit the premises in their respective locations in the event of a fire. Each audience member's focus is on *their* floors and *their* employees. They need to be able to explain only the pertinent information to the individuals that they are responsible for.

He smiled at me and said, "Gotcha, that makes sense."

We then proceeded to separate that single diagram into several visuals, focusing on the floors that would be relevant to the respective supervisors. We simplified the visuals and highlighted only key features that they would need to know (exit routes, etc.). We then applied this formula to his upcoming presentation to prepare a professional, clear, and user-friendly session for his next audience. Voila! New audience, new presentation.

The YOU perspective

Despite the fact that you can only control what you do before, during, and after your presentation, the reality is that your desired outcome will depend on your audience. They are the other, large part to the successful presentation equation that cannot be ignored. You are focusing on what you can control in an effort to influence the audience to do, think, or believe something.

A major component of this perspective is shifting the way in which you frame your content. This initially meant shifting from explaining features or functions, to emphasizing benefits. Nowadays, we can broaden its application to focusing less on causes, more on effects. This signals to the audience that you understand them and have taken the time to outline how they will be positively impacted. More on this in Chapter Five, *Content Structure*.

The prevailing approach proven to be effective in connecting with people and influencing them is through the "you" perspective. Many people tend to view their purpose looking inward initially. A sort of "What am I supposed to do/include?" or "I need to do really well in this presentation" reaction. This process is called the "me" perspective, which is the default programming for most of us. Fortunately for you, your audience will be comprised of *most of us*. So, you would be better served to switch that perspective around to: "What would *they* like me to include?", "What content will most benefit *them*?", "What are *their* needs," or "It's very important that they understand this information." A past experience might help do this point justice.

I was coaching a Sales and Marketing executive for a large appliance company in the U.K. They were in the midst of presenting their latest marketing plan to their company's board of directors. This executive reached out to me because his last presentation wasn't very well received. He wanted me to review his latest presentation a few days before he had to present it to the board. Upon reviewing his presentation with him, we immediately discovered that his presentation was "Me" focused. It was chock-full of statements like, "according to my research," "In my opinion," "I'm very confident that we should," and finally, "I'd be happy to take the lead on this strategy." As we went through his material and presentation, I could see on his face that he was sincere in all of his statements and that he genuinely felt that it was solely his strategy, based on his research, and that he should be the one to see it through. The problem was from the board's perspective, he would appear as attempting to force-feed it to them.

I explained to him, "All of your information and facts are correct and accurate, but we would need to package them and frame them differently to maximize reception."

"What do you mean?" was his response.

I then asked, "What's your desired outcome of this presentation?"

He said, "I want to do better than last time."

I probed a little further and asked, "What does that look like?"

He said, "Well, they should accept my strategy and it shouldn't be that complicated."

"Right!" I said. "Your desired outcome is for the board to determine that the marketing strategy that you've presented has a high probability of success."

He then exclaimed, "That's right! And I should be the one to carry it out."

I told him, "I understand." Then I said, "Now that we've established your desired outcome, does it really matter if the board members believe that it was your plan? Will they possibly find out some other way?"

He quickly replied, "Yes, probably."

I said, "Okay, great. So, let's change the perspective and ensuing language that you are going to use."

The most effective approach for this scenario would be to present the information as clearly and as unbiased as possible. We restructured his presentation to reflect an objective view. And we changed all of the "me, my, and I" statements to more neutral language, such as "The research indicates..." and "Since it's been established..." Now, the crucial insight that I shared with this client was that although you may be tempted to give your personal or professional opinion because you are so certain that it will work, don't. Upon completion of your presentation, you will ask the audience if they have any questions. At this point, they will likely ask your opinion either directly or indirectly, and you'll have a chance to share your viewpoint. This way, you'll have presented yourself as an unbiased, genuine professional whose intent is to provide the board with enough accurate information for them to make an informed decision. They will appreciate your time, effort, and intention. Further, you will become more trusted and valued as a team member. It took some convincing, but he agreed. Ultimately, he achieved his desired outcome and was now "running point" on his major marketing plan. We had a follow-up conversation a short time afterwards. He told me that he learned a valuable lesson from our experience: Up until collaborating with me, he had been trying to convince others of what they should do via presentations. He has since learned that if you simply explain your reasoning in a clear and concise structure, the audience members are more likely to arrive at your conclusion.

Chapter Three

Presentation Logistics

Once you have determined your desired outcome and your audience, your next step to executing a successful professional presentation is to consider the particulars. By that I mean, the physical parameters that you must adhere to such as: time limit, location, and resources. These details might seem like afterthoughts in preparation for your presentation, but they are necessities. Many seasoned presenters ask logistical questions like a reflex upon being tasked with a professional presentation. Questions such as, "How much time will I have?", "Will I be presenting in our conference room like last time?", or "Will I have access to a projector/screen/white board/ etc.?" I can't tell you how many presentations I've seen get cut off due to timing. And rushing to finish is one of the most irritating experiences for your audience.[1] The common remark from the presenter is: "I didn't even get to my strongest point." You can guess how effective those types of presentations are.

Key Presentation Logistical Information

1. Time
2. Space/Location
3. Resources/Equipment

It's About Time

There's a huge difference between a presentation intended for 10 minutes and one intended for 30 minutes. The first step is to identify how much time you'll have to present. Once you know the timeframe that you're working with, consider subtracting approximately 15 - 20% for questions afterwards. The remaining time becomes your window to comfortably plan your presentation delivery. More often than not, presentations tend to be overloaded with information as opposed to underloaded. In fact, cramming too much information is one of the leading causes of failed presentations.[2,3,4] We'll explore this issue more in the next chapter (*Content Selection*) but for now, keep in mind that time goes quickly when you're presenting. Getting cut off is a sign of poor preparation. When you're designing your presentation and organizing your content, knowing how much time that you'll have to comfortably speak about your topic is essential to the planning process.

Timing Advice

Less is more. Time to spare is better than rushing or being motioned to wrap up your presentation. Most professionals in your audience will appreciate brevity and conciseness. You can always extend the question period if you run short and address any outstanding concerns or points. And remember: you're not "running short," you are "ahead of schedule."

Location, location, location

Where you will be presenting can impact your comfort level and, ultimately, your performance. If you're presenting in a room that you're familiar with, concerns such as where to stand and what your vantage point will be may be a non-issue. However, if you are presenting in unfamiliar territory, it's a good idea to scope out the venue first and get a lay of the land. I've seen very experienced presenters stumble and falter when faced with a change of scenery.

As a university lecturer and curriculum developer, I have attended my fair share of presentations in academia. One afternoon, I was informed that, later on in the week, I would be expected to attend a presentation by a former colleague of mine. The next day, I spoke to my colleague at our photocopier. He mentioned that he would be presenting in the usual place, which was the boardroom beside our offices. So, on that Friday, as the presentation time was approaching, I was packing up my belongings and preparing to head to the presentation. I walked to my colleague's office to wish him luck, but he was gone. His administrative assistant kindly informed me that he wasn't presenting in our boardroom, but in the lecture hall downstairs instead. I recall not feeling overly concerned about the change. I didn't think much of it.

As I entered the lecture hall, I noticed that there were about five times the amount of people in attendance, which probably accounted for the change in venue. I found my seat quickly and my colleague began his presentation. I remember seeing him on stage, struggling with his technology. There was a compatibility issue at first with the projector. Then, as he began to speak, he was stumbling over his words. I could sense a great deal of hesitation and a lack of confidence. He kept referring to the clock and his slides behind him. He was pacing around on stage as he was speaking, before he realized that he was blocking the audience's view of his visuals. He then moved almost out of sight for the remainder of his presentation. It was a pull on the collar "yikes" sigh moment for all of us in the audience, as he struggled to recover. The audience was so focused on his behavior that they missed most of the content they were meant to absorb.

When we got back to the office, I asked him to grab a cup of coffee and he eagerly agreed. I said to him that the presentation must have been a rough go: a last-minute venue change, and a much larger audience than anticipated. He told me that it was his own fault. He was alerted the previous day that the venue had to be changed due to the increase in audience size, and he didn't bother to check out the new location. He said he only asked one question about the lecture hall: "Does it have a projector?" When he learned that it did, he figured that he could make do with whatever else there was.

As it turned out, he couldn't. He said that the tech wasn't even the biggest problem, nor the size of the audience. It was the stage that threw him for a loop. He didn't know where to stand, if he was supposed to move around using the whole stage area, or if anyone could even see him. All of these mishaps could have been avoided by taking a three-minute trip to the venue and checking it out. In this case, the minor cost of time could have yielded a major benefit of comfort and performance.

Critical Considerations on Presentation Location

- Will there be a podium or lectern to use?
- Where will I stand? Will I be able to move around?
- Where will my audience be in relation to me?
- What will be my view of the audience?

Available Resources

The final logistical information that you'll want to know prior to your upcoming professional presentation is what resources will be available to you. Typically, this means technology, but not always. Knowing whether or not you'll be provided with a microphone is important to know, and if it's stationary, attached to a podium, or portable. Most commonly, presenters will use visual aids and Audio/Video support (slide deck). You should determine what type of technology is compatible with the venue's set up. A few of the more notable tech questions and concerns are listed below. In recent research on presentations, 61% of audience members reported that the presentation was "flawed" because the presenter didn't know how to use their equipment.[1]

There is also the possible situation where the use of a white board and markers is needed to track a discussion or explain a concept. If this is the case and the venue is not equipped with these materials, you're faced with a decision. You can request or make arrangements for them to be available, but plan to go on without them just in case. Alternatively, you can adapt your presentation to not require certain resources, though this may take some design manoeuvring. The main points here are to not take anything for granted and to confirm what you will have at your disposal.

Test the Tech

As a best practice, the presenter should arrive approximately a half hour early to begin setting up. Since technology is not always your best friend, you should immediately test the equipment that you'll be using upon arrival. Make sure that the video, audio, internet, compatibility, etc. is functioning properly prior to your presentation. In the case that it's malfunctioning, you'll have some time to request tech support and prepare accordingly. You may have to rearrange some components of your presentation, or improvise by using what's available. Either way, it's better to find out if there is a problem sooner, rather than later. Confirming that your technology is working will also add to your confidence level while presenting. If your technology does work well and there are no issues, you can spend some time warming up the audience in advance.

Critical Considerations on Presentation Resources

- Does the venue have a projector that I can use?
- Is the tech set up compatible with HDMI?
- Is the venue equipped with a computer or should I bring my own device?
- Will I have a microphone (handheld or clip-on)?
- Will there be a presentation pointer/clicker available?
- How can I gain access to the WiFi?

Side note: I always recommend having your visual aids (slides) prepared and readily available through multiple avenues (i.e. USB, cloud, etc.) just in case technology fails. For example, if the internet goes out and you had your presentation prepared in Google Slides, have a back up on a portable USB drive. Also, it never hurts to bring your own remote-controlled clicker with fresh batteries. And if you're using a white board with dry-erase markers, make sure that they work!

Elevator Pitch Scenario

Although an elevator pitch is not exactly a professional presentation, it does share some of the same qualities, and since I get asked about them frequently, I think it's useful to provide some insight. I define an "elevator pitch" as an enclosed situation, whereby you have only a brief period of time (approximately 30 – 45 seconds) to convince another person that you can offer them something of value. The goal for the speaker is to persuade the listener to arrange more time to converse. The best-case scenario would be to come away with an agreement or commitment from the listener, but oftentimes, it's not realistic. For the sake of practicality, the speaker is aiming to gain enough interest from the listener that a future meeting is arranged and/or contact information is exchanged.

Challenges

The challenges here begin with the fact that the speaker likely won't have any visual aids on hand, so they must orally present their content effectively. They, most likely, will not have anything prepared for this particular encounter, as it is spontaneous. They have limited face-time with their listener, forcing them to organize and make quick decisions on their content mentally, while trying to deliver effectively. All of this with the compounding effect of adrenaline flowing because they will probably not get a second chance at speaking with this individual.

Treatment/remedy

The best path to success is to acknowledge these challenges and then proceed accordingly. First, take five seconds to inhale deeply and exhale slowly. In the meantime, organize only two points in your mind. Point number one is: What particular value does your company, product, or service offer? Point number two is: How would this individual benefit from engaging with your company, product, or service? After you exhale, greet the individual politely and then begin explaining your points to them (see example outline below). You only have one presentation goal in this case: to present your two points as clearly as possible. Be prepared; the listener might have other commitments or items on their mind, or might not be interested in your services. However, if you present yourself and your case respectfully and clearly, you should hold your head high as a professional!

You'll be shocked at how easy this becomes once you begin.

Example Outline of an Elevator Pitch

1. (Greeting and opening) "Hi. My name's _____ . I'm an admirer of your work..."
2. (Lead into your first point....) "My company, _____, has just developed a product that's so unique..."
3. (Followed by your second point...) "I know that you're somewhat of an expert on _____ and I'm curious if you think that it would be beneficial for someone like yourself?" (After they respond, explain what you anticipate are benefits for them).
4. (Closing question) "Would you be opposed to continuing this conversation sometime?"

Chapter Four

Content Selection

The "Rush to Start" Trap

Please, please, please do not fall into the "rush to start" trap. Many presenters fall prey to the temptation of starting to create slides beginning with whatever content is on their mind at the time. They simply continue to add more information as it comes to them. They then realize, or sometimes do not realize, that they have too many slides, so they proceed to cram more information into fewer slides. Then, they scramble to organize the presentation at the last-minute right before delivery. They have essentially said to themselves, "I know what I need to do," then skipped the goals establishment, audience analysis, and logistics considerations. As a result, their audience becomes the people who requested this presentation, their desired outcome and goals are merely to get through the presentation, and their logistical considerations are: "I'll figure it out when I get there."

These compounding choices lead to the creation of a piecemeal, Frankenstein-like presentation with very little organization. It results in a large breadth of content, but very little depth of content. Basically, the presenter has decided not to focus on any particular goals; rather, they are hopeful that the audience will be able to pick out the value from the smorgasbord of content. This effect is like building a house for someone without bothering to consider how they'd like it to turn out or what materials might be included. You might start laying bricks, then remember that they need a door, so you just add one in somewhere. Then you remember that they probably like windows and you backtrack to make a window or two. As you can imagine, it's highly unlikely that a client will be satisfied with what you've produced. It's more likely that they will feel overlooked, undervalued, and/or frustrated.

Content Selection Process

Of all of the components that work together to make the optimal professional presentation, the question of which content to include and which to omit may pose the greatest challenge. The answer here is rarely black and white. At some point, you will have to make a judgment call. However, the good news is that there are a few safeguards that you can put in place to help you filter and narrow down your content selection. By this point in the process, you should have a firm grasp on your desired outcome, your audience, and your presentation logistics. The content selection process is as follows:

1. Become the expert
2. Separate content into three groups
3. Time high priority content
4. Prioritize midrange content (sometimes)
5. Time midrange content (sometimes)

Becoming the Expert

Most likely, you will already be familiar and well acquainted with the information that you'll be presenting. But in the event that you are not, you must make yourself knowledgeable. Not just because you will need to demonstrate your expertise and understanding, but more importantly because you'll need to have everything on the table before you start sorting through content. If you don't take the time to familiarize yourself with all of the relevant information on your topic, you risk omitting a crucial piece of content in your presentation. You also risk looking foolish or unprepared in the event that someone questions you regarding the content that you *should* know. The good news is that completing this process will often lead to a boost in presentation confidence. Presenters who have a more comprehensive understanding of their material tend to project more confidence and appear less nervous when delivering. As you might expect this level of comfort will have a positive impact on your presentation.

Once you have achieved this level of familiarity with your presentation topic, you will come to the realization that you cannot present everything. There simply isn't enough time to share all of the information that you have on the topic with your audience. You'll need to start the paring down process.

Content Evaluation

The simplest, most effective way to begin determining what your presentation should consist of is to look at the full spectrum and then begin to sort. First, ask yourself: Which content is of little or no use to my audience? Then move on to: What do they absolutely *need* to know? The remainder of your information will be labelled "might be useful to the audience," and will likely be your largest section. What you will end up with is three categories of information. You absolutely must know your audience and goals in order to complete this process effectively. See the visual below.

High Priority Content (Must include)	Midrange Content (Might be useful to the audience)	Low Value Content (Comfortably exclude)

Visit www.professionalpresentationservices.com to access the free supplementary resources

Time "High Priority Content"

The next step is to make a bulleted list from the information that the audience absolutely needs to know. Then, considering only this "high priority" content, you'll need to give some thought and predict how much time it will take you to effectively communicate these points to your audience. Disregard the organization of the content for now. Your focus should be on labelling each of the bulleted content with an accurate estimate of time (i.e., Issues with current service model = 4 – 4.5 min). At first, you might need to time yourself while you rehearse, but as you become more experienced, you'll be able to estimate your delivery time more accurately.

If the amount of presentation time aligns with the amount of time it will take you to deliver your "High priority content," then that's all of the content that you will include. You may then move on to the structure and organization stage of the process (Chapter Five, *Presentation Structuring & Organization*). However, if you anticipate having excess time after including only your "high priority" content, which is often the case, you'll need to make some decisions regarding what else to include. Before long, you'll find yourself only needing two categories, "high priority content" and "midrange content," as you'll instinctively cross-off less relevant content.

Prioritize "Midrange Content"

The next step is to take a minute and reflect on your desired outcome, goals, and audience. You'll want to make a list out of your "midrange content" pile. Then begin to order and prioritize the content in this category from most to least anticipated impact and/or value. Typically, these points will be supplemental benefits, evidence, or other considerations pertaining to the topic of your presentation. This is also the point at which you can begin to spot the more persuasive content, or consider how to use some of this content in a persuasive way (refer to Chapter Five, *Presentation Structuring & Organization*) to influence your desired outcome.

Time "Midrange Content"

You'll need to estimate how long your midrange content points will take to present. This will help you determine how many and which points to include while staying within your timeframe. The more excess time that you have, the more content points you can include. But keep in mind that there will likely be a question-and-answer period, wherein the audience will address any relevant information that was not mentioned. So, avoid putting too much pressure on yourself, and leave yourself some time. There's no need to feel rushed.

The Selection Curve

The recipe for success when deciding which content to include is explained above. But it's not written in stone. As you become more comfortable presenting, you will be able to read the audience more accurately and tailor your presentation more toward them. If you've completed the process correctly, you'll have much more knowledge and information than you have planned to present. This provides you with an enormous advantage. You will present the most meaningful content, you will design visual aids to complement your valuable and complex content, and you will have much more to offer in your back pocket, if needed. Don't be afraid to throw out another statistic or data point off-script if you feel that the audience would benefit from hearing it. But keep your presentation goals in mind at all times. Keep in mind the logistical constraints that all presentations are under.

In the end, you'll have to make a choice: try to scratch the surface of all the content, which leads to little retention and even less impact, or spend your time going deeper on selective, high value content. You won't be able to adequately include everything, and attempting to would be a fool's errand.

Research on presentation failures demonstrates that the most annoying aspect of any presentation is "the main point being obscured by too much irrelevant detail." This complaint was followed by, "contained too much material to absorb before moving on to the next point."[1]

Danger… Information Overload

Just recently, I was hired to consult on a large U.S. based company's new product launch. When I met the gentleman that would be presenting, I asked if he had started designing his presentation already, or whether he was still establishing his foundation. To my surprise, he had shared with me eight pages of text, which turned out to be his entire script. I asked him what he had planned to do with this information and he responded: "Read it! Of course."

Reading to the audience is a foolproof way to avoid forgetting anything of importance. The issue, of course, is that when you're reading, the audience is likely snoring or checking their phones. I explained this to the individual and added that when you read to your audience during your presentation, they will absorb very little of what you say. They may give you the benefit of the doubt for the first minute or so, but eventually they will tune you out. However, if you deliver your most valuable, high priority content, while focusing on the needs of your audience, they will absorb much more information. He nodded, as if to signal that he understood the logic behind my explanation, but I sensed trepidation in his agreement, so I asked what was on his mind.

He said: "I would still hate for the audience to leave curious about something that I forgot to cover."

I responded, "Trust me… If they really want to know something that you haven't said, they'll ask."

The moral of the story: focus on presenting your high priority content and accomplishing your presentation goals. DO NOT read. Reading to the audience is a leading cause of audience frustration because the approach is often perceived as dry, impersonal, and boring.[1]

Iceberg of Wisdom

Presenters are portrayed as experts in a specialized area or on a specific topic. Which means that presenters are expected to possess three to four times more information and knowledge than their audience. So, even though you will only be presenting on a fraction of the information that you have, you should be prepared to speak more on the topic. Think of yourself like an iceberg; your presentation reflects about 20 - 25% of all of the content that you have examined. The remainder is underneath the surface. Fortunately for you, if you've followed the steps outlined in this chapter, during the content selection process, you will be able to amass a stockpile of information to have at your fingertips. Which means that even though you will not be including the previously deemed "excess information" in your presentation, it can still be quite useful. Print it or have it within arm's reach during your presentation. This strategy will enable you to respond to questions more accurately in the event that more detail is requested. Not to mention the optics of the situation. You will appear more professional when you are prepared to answer a question that you've anticipated. The cherry on top is that having these notes handy will actually make you more comfortable and confident. You are not expected to know everything. You are expected to know the "essential content + supporting details" of your presentation and where to find the "excess information" quickly.

More Info Available

If you find yourself in a time crunch when discussing a main point, or you'd like to elaborate on some interesting content that's connected to your main point, consider using one of the "More info available phrases and gambits" below. These are designed to inform your audience that you have more information upon request, but that you've made a calculated decision to focus on the more crucial content. They illustrate to the audience that you've done your homework and are knowledgeable on your topic. They also demonstrate your professionalism in being mindful of the time.

More Info Available Phrases and Gambits

- "There are some interesting details behind this point, but for time's sake we'll move on to...."
- "There is actually a lot of data that factored into this. I'd be happy to circle back later on, if time allows."
- "The main point/result here is **(insert main point)** but there was much data that went into this, so please feel free to ask any questions about the specifics during the Q & A session."
- "I'd be happy to go into more detail on this concept after my presentation. Now, for time's sake, I'm going to move on to **(next point)**."
- "There is some interesting information and evidence behind this. Perhaps if there's some time at the end, I can elaborate."
- "There are actually some additional factors at play here, but for the sake of this presentation, we're going to focus on **(key content/point)**."
- "This information is a summary. I'd be happy to speak about the particulars with you afterwards if you'd like."

In the next chapter, you will learn all about the differences between informative and persuasive presentation structuring. However, as you know, by the time you are sifting through and deciding which content to include, you have already determined your desired outcome and established a few presentation goals. During this process, be careful to not include too much compounding content that overstates a point to the audience. There *is* such a thing as over-arguing. Think about someone trying to convince you to do something that you've already agreed to. It can be frustrating or irritating. Decide which information will be most impactful, aim for the three or four most powerful key points, then keep the rest of your information on hand. Remember: information overload is a leading cause of presentation disasters.[1,2]

Paralysis by Analysis

This is a recurring theme throughout the professional presentation framework. Thinking and planning ahead, along with accurately anticipating, play a crucial role in the process of creating a professional presentation. Furthermore, it's very important that you do your best investigative work to include the most critical content. However, when sifting through content, you'll eventually reach the point of diminishing returns. At this point, you'd be wise to move on to the next step in the process. When selecting content, the most essential steps are determining what can definitely be removed or omitted, and what needs to be included. 90% of content selection is being confident in those decisions. I've seen presenters sink hours and days into going back and forth on content selection. The reality is that, after a certain point, your efforts are best focused elsewhere. Know when to move on.

Chapter Five

Presentation Structuring & Organization

Each presentation is unique and, as such, requires an individualized structure. Unfortunately, cookie cutter structures don't fit most presentations and, even when they do, they leave much to be desired. But hope is not lost! By following the framework and process outlined in this guide, you will systematically assemble your professional presentation with the optimal structure for your individual circumstances. This chapter of the guide contains structures, tools, and techniques to optimize your professional presentation. Furthermore, this section has been refined and distilled for easy absorption and integration.

Preselecting Your Structure

Using an established cookie cutter approach might seem like a good idea at first, as it may appear to save you time and align with your content. However, some issues inevitably arise. One is that not all of your high value content can be easily compartmentalized. Another is that you may find one section of your presentation overloaded, while another is too light. You may be left second-guessing yourself and feeling like you've missed something. You want to build your equation around your factors, not try to cram your factors into a pre-set equation. This process is like trying to jam a square peg into a round hole. Instead, carve the hole around your peg because each peg is unique, and you are the foremost authority on the high value content.

Stick to Your Guns

Personally, this is my favourite part of crafting a professional presentation because it's like preparing a game plan in advance of a big game. You get to decide the order of the content that you're going to reveal and the best way to outline key concepts. I call this process "unpacking concepts" or "unfolding content" for the audience, and it is a thing of beauty when performed effectively. There are an infinite number of approaches to organize your presentation and some approaches are better than others. But what's most important is that once you choose a structure, you stick with it. You can still present effectively with an odd or suboptimal structure, although it's unnecessary. However, if you change your direction midway, even to a more suitable structure for your content, it will detract from the overall effectiveness of the presentation by creating audience confusion. The audience are left wondering what's going on with the presentation instead of anticipating what will be said next or making connections with other information. In the end, organizing your presentation boils down to designing a sequence to present your content that will be easiest for the audience to follow.[1]

Note: You should organize your content only after you have decided the details and information that the presentation will include. If you attempt to do both simultaneously, you risk including useless information and omitting valuable information, not to mention wasting time. Follow the framework.

Presentation Structure Overview

1. Introduction
2. Body Content
3. Conclusion

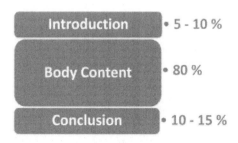

Introduction	• 5 - 10 %
Body Content	• 80 %
Conclusion	• 10 - 15 %

As an overview, the professional presentation design framework consists of the following elements: introduction, body, and conclusion. Avoid overcomplicating your design and resist the urge to immediately begin feeding information to the audience. This structure of communicating information has been successful on every level and has been optimized for presentation success. Think about the last book that you read or movie that you saw: nearly all structured communication follows this pattern. First, the setting, background information, and/or scenario is outlined to ensure a shared understanding. Next, changes, challenges, events, action/reaction, etc. and their potential impact are explained in a logical sequence. Finally, the key content is recapped, and the main message/resolution is reiterated to the audience. People have been conditioned to process information in this particular sequence and have become quite proficient at doing so.

However, it's important to note when you're ready to design your professional presentation, the starting point is *not* the introduction. In fact, it is the body. Once you have structured the content of the body, move on to the conclusion, and save the introduction for last. You'll need to begin organizing your body content first because it will have implications on both your introduction and conclusion. As you read on, you will find that the structures for introductions and conclusions are fairly consistent across all professional presentations. And they're both influenced by the organization of the body.

The Body

"Form follows function," as correctly stated by the great American architect, Louis Sullivan. In other words, the structure of your presentation will depend on your desired outcome and presentation goals. Recall (Chapter One) that there are two general but distinct purposes when presenting: to inform or to persuade. If your desired outcome is for your audience to become more aware or informed of something, then your presentation is informative. Persuasive presentations also use information as a means of influencing the audience. If your desired outcome is for your audience to do something or believe something, then your presentation is persuasive. The order in which you structure your information within your presentation (content organization) will begin to take shape as you progress through the process outlined in this chapter. To complete the process successfully, a series of clear decisions based on critical thinking must be made. As a result, whether you're presenting a case study, problem-solution scenario, or quarterly update, this process will customize the optimal structure for your unique presentation.

Body Content Organization Process

1. Review all selected content points
2. Identify commonalities amongst your selected content
3. Review the five "Systems of Organization"
4. Group similar content together (aim for 2 – 4 groups); these become sections
5. Determine the most effective sequence to present your sections

Systems of Organization

At this point, you have a clear list of content points that you've decided to include in your presentation which meets your timeframe. Carefully examine each of your bulleted list of content points to determine if there are any connections between them. This process will enable you to group multiple points together into separate categories. For example, if some of your content points pertain to geographical areas or districts, you might consider grouping points by location. These categories or groups will eventually become distinct sections of your presentation body (aim for 2 – 4). Unfortunately, due to the uniqueness of each professional presentation, there is no plug-and-play structure that I could provide in good conscience. However, I can provide you with the five most effective and practical organizational systems that will adapt to your needs and circumstances.[2]

1. Chronological

The first option to organize the body content of your presentation is across time. Time is universally relatable and understandable. You may choose to arrange your content across a timeline, from earliest to most recent. Then, during the delivery of your presentation, you will essentially be walking your audience through the events that have unfolded in chronological order. This system of organization has been widely successful across a range of presentations, and is most frequently used when presenting project details, updates, and case studies.

2. Locational or Positional

The next option is to group or compartmentalize your content by location or positionally. Location is also very relatable to your audience. This system of organization can be used if your content is collected in a few, definable geographical areas. Also, in the case that you are presenting a diagram of a particular product, for example, you can use the overview of the product as a frame of reference and then progress in a downward direction explaining the various content and components. A few notable uses for this system include: territorial reports, product development, or sales projections.

3. Categorical

This option is to group or compartmentalize your content by a common characteristic or shared, main theme. You will end up with separate categories of content and will then be able to choose an order to present them. Popular organizational systems such as problem/solution, features/benefits, and comparison matrices are all forms of categorical organization. Many technology companies follow this organizational system during new product launches. They might group their content into Product Design, Usability, Hardware, and Compatibility, for example. Or, in the case of a competitor analysis, you might group content by product or service.

4. Alphabetical or Acronym

This option also groups your content by common attribute or main theme. Once the content is grouped, label each group by its shared attribute or theme. From there, arrange the first letter of each label to make a word or term. This organizational structure may take some creativity on your part, but can be very effective from an audience's perspective. An example of this would be to present a SWOT analysis of a company, whereby the presenter will explain that the acronym SWOT represents strengths, weaknesses, opportunities, and threats, then sequentially unpack each.

5. Hierarchy

This option requires grouping or compartmentalizing your content pertaining to levels of significance or authority. This structure might take the visual form of a pyramid shape, mind map, or flow chart. It illustrates the different levels of content, as well as their relationship with each other. For example, a professional presentation focusing on the restructuring of an organization would benefit from this organizational system. The presenter would begin by revealing the big picture of the hierarchical structure, then focus in on the individual aspects that are affected. This organizational system is also utilized in investment pitches and presentations as it enables the presenters to showcase the entire infrastructure and highlight the value where applicable.

Troubleshooting Organization

Sometimes, your content is not easily connected or grouped together and many presenters rack their brains trying to make connections. This is an unnecessary and time-consuming endeavour. In order to troubleshoot properly, refer back to your entire list of included content points. Read them all again once more so that they are fresh in your mind. Then review the five types of organization: Chronological, Positional, Categorical, Alphabetical, Hierarchal. At this point, a light bulb will likely turn on and you can begin crafting your organization of content.

If not, and you're still stuck, you should focus on two or three of your content points and ask yourself: How are these similar? How are these different? You may find that your content points are similar or different due to a variable that had previously been overlooked. That variable will turn into your grouping label. You can use this strategy with different subsets of your content points to find a commonality or comparison.

Finally, the last bullet in the chamber is to zoom in and/or zoom out when attempting to group your content points. People often prefer to absorb content in a particular manner. Your content will be organized with this in mind. I've been contacted many times to solve this exact problem, whereby the presenter is having difficulty grouping their content into sections. It's often a case of "not seeing the forest through the trees" or being too close to the content to see the separation lines. You may be thinking too micro or too macro. You may be thinking too specific or too general.

Troubleshooting in Action

I once received a panicked call from a medical supply company in Texas that was having this very issue. The representative explained some of his content and had become frustrated because his presentation was important and he didn't want to appear as if he "just threw some data together and hope it sticks," to use his words.

After carefully listening to his content points, I suggested: "It seems like you should organize your content positionally, by location."

"I already thought of that, and I can't because all of our activity is in Northern Texas," he said hopelessly, as if he was burned out.

I replied calmly, "Ok, let's say that you're right."

"I am right," he said, sharply.

I said, "Okay. You're right. Northern Texas is still an awfully large area, though. I'm sure that you can separate your content by position within it. Then you can organize your presentation by sequencing the counties or districts."

There was a pause for about three seconds on the call, and I thought that I had missed something obvious and he had hung up in frustration.

I was just about to ask, "Are you still there?" when he chimed in: "Uh, yeah., Actually, I think that would work. That might work well. I guess I should have thought of that before I bothered you. Next time I'll zoom in."

I didn't quite know what he meant at first by "zoom in." But I now understand it as a means to view your content from different angles or through a different lens to eventually find your optimal structure. Fun fact: his presentation ended up being a success and he has been in touch with me ever since. I still get a Christmas card from him every year.

Transitioning Between Sections & Signposting

Your groupings of content will end up becoming the sections of your presentation body. This guide refers to content groupings and their ordering as your organization. As you're presenting, the time will come to tie up one of the sections and transition into another. This task might seem easy at face value, but it can become a stumbling awkward situation. Not to mention the research indicates that signposting for the audience the beginnings and endings of distinct sections improves members' attention and comprehension.[3,4] The following list of transition phrases has been compiled for your benefit:

Transition/Signposting Phrases and Gambits

- Okay, so we've just finished examining/ looking at **(insert topic/section)**. Now, we're going to move onto **(insert next topic/section)**.
- Alright, so we've explained what **(insert product name)** is. Now let's discuss its benefits.
- This leads us to my next point… **(insert next topic/section)**.
- This brings us to the final section of my presentation today… **(insert next topic/section)**.

Informative Perspective

Informative presentations are unbiased and objective. Presenters are similar to teachers in that they are positioned to share knowledge and information with no other agenda in mind. They are meant to be neutral facilitators of information.

When the desired outcome of your professional presentation is for the audience to become more informed or knowledgeable about your topic (as in a quarterly update, shareholders' meeting, employee address, etc.), the process of designing your presentation will begin by establishing your presentation goals. The following are some questions to help you begin:

- What do they need/want to know?
- Which information is most valuable for them?
- What do you intend for them to do with this information, if anything?
- How will this information help them?
- What are their next steps, if any?

New Tech, Anyone?

An experience that captures the essence of this tactic involves me being asked to consult on an informative presentation for a large, nutritional company. The situation was that the company was changing a key program and piece of software that thousands of their employees were using on a weekly basis. The desired outcome was to educate their employees to use this new technology efficiently. In this case, it would not benefit the audience to have explained why the change in technology was made or how much it would cost the company. The answers to those questions would not help the employees adapt to the new technology more efficiently. Presenting excess information often creates more confusion and leads to a colossal waste of time. Instead, we focused on explaining how to use the new technology in the most common situations that their employees would encounter.

Then we focused on how to troubleshoot the technology in case of malfunction. And finally, we revealed the newly created in-house tech support team. We determined that the best way to help shorten the learning curve with the new technology, and improve employee performance, was to focus on these presentation goals. We tracked the amount of tech support requests for three months following the presentation. That was our measuring stick for success. Ultimately, the presentation was a success because we achieved our desired outcome. Afterwards, the employees reported being able to seamlessly adapt to the new technology and the tech support team reported that new support requests were at an all-time low!

Bridging the Gap

Next, you'll need to determine your bridging point: when you'll share the new information. This process can be tricky and will require some consideration. If you overestimate how much your audience knows going in, you risk confusing them. Underestimate their knowledge base, and they'll become bored, as you waste time reiterating what they already know. An effective audience analysis is in order (refer to Chapter Two, *Interpreting Your Audience*). You must accurately determine how much the audience already knows about the information that you plan to present. Once you have a good estimate as to the extent of their knowledge, you'll be able to minimize time spent recapping. As a rule of thumb, spend about 15 – 20 seconds, or three – four sentences, bringing the audience up to speed.

Now that your presentation goals (end point) have been established and your audience (starting point) has been assessed, you can begin to design your presentation. Your next task is to bridge this gap within the allotted time frame, using the resources that you have at your disposal. Near the beginning, consider quickly recapping some key content that your audience members are expected to know (possibly highlighted in your pre-presentation document, Chapter Two). This approach will lay the foundation to take the audience with you through your presentation.

Since you've already removed all of the nonessential information, you then must choose one of the five organizations systems listed above to shape your content. A common organization structure for informative presentations is chronological as it easily accommodates case-study, updates, reviews, and other formats when events occur across a timeline (action, then reaction, and so on). This format is very logical and is user-friendly for your audience's understanding. Although it's not universal and won't always fit with your presentation content.

Organizing Opportunities

I can recall a great example of organization when I was collaborating with a COO of a tech company in Silicon Valley. She had been tasked with presenting three potential opportunities to her superiors. As we discussed and diagnosed her presentation, we determined that her desired outcome was for her superiors to make the best decision possible for their company.

In order to make the best decision, they would need to be made aware of the most accurate, up-to-date, and relevant content. These points became her presentation goals. In this case, we decided to group her content by opportunity, and then within each opportunity, use the same structure of anticipated timeline, cost, and benefit. This organization and structure of content would have been sufficient on its own, but we decided to go one step further and rank the opportunities in terms of potential benefit. The opportunity that would have the most significant impact on her company but potentially yield the most return was set for last; the second most impactful opportunity was explained second. Then the opportunity that was the least intrusive and risky was her lead. This structure was very effective in comprehensively informing her superiors via a well-organized presentation. Ultimately, her superiors were able to make an informed, confident decision thanks to her efforts and she demonstrated that she can step up and deliver when called upon— like a professional.

In this case, the structure that was implemented was dependent upon the degree of company benefit. Sometimes, the method that you choose might be considered subjective, and that's certainly true when using vague terms like "positive outcome." However, please remember that when you get to this level of thought and organization, it's almost like splitting hairs. The hard truth regarding informative presentations is that effective organization is rarely praised, but disorganization can be spotted from a mile away, and can derail a presentation in no time.

Creating Persuasion

When our desired outcome is to influence our audience's behaviour or mindset, it's a persuasive presentation. Persuasive presentations are almost always supported with facts and information, yet they are not considered informative. Persuasive presentations are slightly more complicated because you are not merely conveying information; you are shaping it and organizing it to achieve a desired impact. The content that you choose to include and the order in which you choose to unpack it will build toward influencing your audience to agree with you or to change their behaviour as a result.

Persuasive Presentation Overview

Effective persuasive presentation structures share the same basic qualities of informative structures through to the content selection stage. So, you will still be establishing your foundation and selecting your content, though you may choose slightly different "midrange value content". Furthermore, persuasive presentations utilize the same organizational systems as informative (outlined earlier). However, there are a couple of changes at this point in the process. First, your groups of content are ordered strategically to influence the audience in a specific way. Typically, the final content or point that you present is your most significant. Secondly, the content within each section or grouping may be altered in some fashion (built-up or downplayed) to impact the audience's interpretation. For example, you may choose to expand on the benefits of a service, because you want the audience to interpret more value. The organizational process for body content is outlined below.

Body Content Organization Process – Persuasive Presentation

1. Review all selected content points

   a. Consider adjusting the display of content for persuasive purposes
2. Identify commonalities and similarities of your selected content
3. Groups similar content together (aim for 2 – 4 groups); these become sections
   a. Integrate modes of persuasion to increase influence
4. Choose logical sequence to present your sections
   a. Arrange your sections for maximum impact

Customizing Content within Sections

There are many techniques that you can integrate into your content that work together as powerful tools to influence your audience. Next, you'll find the proven methods and patterns of persuasion that can be utilized along with suggestions for best use. As you read on, you may find that you gravitate to some more than others and that's fine. Some are more preferable depending on the situation, but the overall awareness of these modes and techniques will help you to select the most effective tools for the job.

The Showcase Method

Over the years, I've developed and refined a unique, formulaic process to persuade an audience that I have dubbed *The Showcase Method*. This method can be applied repeatedly within the same presentation to produce astounding results. First, you'll need to identify the component (product/service/company/feature/etc.) of your presentation that you'd like the audience to buy into. Then follow this simple process:

1. Briefly describe the component (Approximately 10% of time)
2. Explain and elaborate on its benefits/advantages/value and

how they can help the audience. Typically, by making their lives easier, safer, or wealthier (Approximately 75% of time)

3. Explain how the component functions, operates, or how it can be used (Approximately 15% of time)

This method is effective because it first brings the audience up to speed on the topic and ensures that all members are on the same page. The audience is left thinking: "Okay, I understand what you're presenting, but why should I be concerned?" Then, it outlines the value that the topic provides at length, in as many ways as possible. At this point, the audience is thinking: "Okay, that sounds great, so how does it work?" Which leads the presenter to explain how the benefits and value are yielded by outlining the functionality or operating process.

The same method can be used to dissuade your audience as well. Step one and three remain the same, but in step two, instead of listing the benefits, advantages, and value, the presenter would outline drawbacks, shortcomings, and disadvantages. Next, you'll read about the classic modes of persuasion. When using *The Showcase Method*, they would be integrated into step two to showcase value.

Three Modes of Persuasion

"Ethos, Pathos, Logos" – Aristotle. In modern English, these translate to credibility, emotion, and logic. These timeless, reigning modes are still utilized to persuade audiences today. Each of these modes can be either used individually or in combination with the others to frame your content. Which will be most effective for your upcoming presentation? That will depend upon your unique presentation foundation (Desired Outcome, Audience, Logistics), but let's first examine how they work.

Ethos = Credibility = Trust

Personal Credibility

"If you don't believe the messenger, you won't believe the message"
- James Kouzes & Barry Posner, *The Leadership Challenge*

For the purposes of persuasive professional presentations, credibility can be separated into three types. First is personal credibility—your credibility. Dress professionally, prepare diligently, and speak confidently, and you will be viewed as a trusted source of information (an expert) by the audience. Obviously, it's advantageous to have an established track record as a reliable professional in advance of your presentation, but it's never too late to start. The reality is, your audience will be more inclined to agree with you if you appear friendly, professional, knowledgeable, and sincere. One of the most effective tools for establishing credibility and building trust with your audience is to demonstrate to them that you understand their situation. A common thought that may be burning in their mind from their history of being an audience member is, "Do you have any idea what I'm faced with?" You can establish a huge amount of credibility, and therefore influence, if you can demonstrate empathy by summarizing their own situation, concerns, and/or upcoming decisions accurately. When performed correctly, this anticipatory technique also has an emotional impact. But, be careful not to go too far out on a limb because if you're mistaken, you'll have demonstrated a lack of understanding toward them and have lost some credibility.

You may be fortunate enough to receive an introduction to your presentation if there is a large or unfamiliar audience. In this case, your accolades and expertise will likely be put on display for the audience before you begin. If so, thank the host for their introduction of you, then proceed on with your presentation. However, in the event that you don't receive a formal introduction, avoid giving one to yourself. This tactic has nothing to do with being humble; the fact of the matter is that, when you start listing your resume, some of your audience members begin mentally checking out. They are far more concerned with what you are about to present to them in the near future than they are with what you've done in the past. If you feel the urge to validate your presence and list your credentials or accolades, check yourself, and shift into focusing on what will help the audience.

Authority as Credibility

This technique accompanies statements, facts, opinions, etc. They're endorsed and supported by established individuals or research published by esteemed professionals, commonly regarded as "experts." Adding authority to your content as a means of persuasion can take many forms, but is most effective when your audience appreciates and respects the source. The methodology here is that if your audience respects the source, and the source supports your presentation goal, the audience is more likely to side with you. Please note that the audience must first recognize who your source of authority is. Then, they must acknowledge the source as someone who is an expert on the subject matter. For example, you wouldn't use a quote from Steve Jobs on the topic of fashion design. Jobs is not considered an expert in fashion; his expertise lies in technology development and business.

Consensus as Credibility

This technique is used to show that many people have already supported your position, or your reasoning is correct because so many people have already indicated it. This approach boils down to there being strength in numbers. The perception is that if many people are currently doing or indicating the same thing, then that or indication is true, valid, or credible. Either their trend is reliable, they are correct, or they have good reason. Depending on your situation, it may be worthwhile to identify any trends or patterns of consensus to use as leverage in your persuasion.

Overall, view credibility like trust. Your goal will be to present your content, argument, suggestions, and yourself as trustworthy. Conversely, failing to build or establish credibility will have the opposite effect. The audience will be left questioning your sources or the validity of your content, instead of considering how they can apply your content in their respective roles. The best presenters maximize their credibility before, during, and after their presentation to increase their influence.

Credibility Phrases and Gambits

- As **(insert expert's name)** repeatedly states **(insert quote)**
- The popular consensus indicates **(insert notion)**
- The majority of experts agree that **(insert concept)**

Pathos = Emotion

Emotional Resolve

Persuading your audience through carefully applied emotional techniques can be accomplished in two ways. The first, similar to personal credibility, is your personal emotion that you emit throughout your presentation. The audience will elicit this emotion from you and mirror you to a degree. In fact, neuroscience has now confirmed what many social psychologists have long believed, that humans are equipped with a part of the brain called "mirror neurons." And just as their name suggests, they are charged with interpreting and then reflecting the emotion.[5] So, if your demeanour is friendly, warm, and respectful, your audience will respond in kind. The research demonstrates that the audience will tend to agree with people whom they like or have positive feelings toward.[6] You don't have to be their best friend, but being respected and considered are also positive feelings for your audience to experience. Take the time to show your appreciation for them throughout your presentation, and you'll find that they will be significantly more receptive and supportive of you. I'll go into more detail on this topic in the "Delivery" sections of this guide (Chapters Seven & Eight), but for now we'll look at building rapport with the audience to improve your desired outcome.

This persuasive technique usually comes quite naturally to extraverts, but it can be a nerve-racking experience for introverts. Diagnose yourself before your presentation, and if your nerves tend to override your operating system, don't force anything more than a smile. Time after time, when an introvert forces themselves too far out of their comfort zone, they get lost at sea. They spend their mental energy trying to focus on their non-verbal and verbal communication at the same time, and they stop focusing on presenting their content to the audience. Present yourself as approachable, respectful, and professional. Nine times out of ten, you'll be well received.

Eliciting Emotional Impact

The second technique is to elicit specific emotions from the audience during your presentation to influence your audience's thoughts and behavior. This feat is achieved through strategic selection of content, visual aids, anecdotes, etc. to evoke a predetermined emotion. Then arranging that content to impact your audience's mindset. The fact is that when people feel differently, they think differently, and their thought process changes.[7] Your mood has a strong impact on your mind, and when you are facing a complex situation, your mood will likely impact our behavior and outcome. For example, we tend to think and act differently when we feel calm and relaxed, compared to when we feel frustrated or threatened. This technique boils down to the presenter stimulating a specific emotion from the audience to influence their mood, then subsequently their actions.

As you try this technique, you'll find that evoking emotion from the audience is quite natural. The challenging part is matching the correct emotion with your desired outcome. Keep in mind that using emotions to motivate decisions is a lot like using tools to build a table. You wouldn't use a hammer to split a piece of wood equally. You'd use a saw. So, make sure that you're using the right tool for the job, to achieve your desired outcome.

Fear & Decision Making

Fear is the most impactful emotion used in persuasive presentations. Specifically, the two most significant fears are fear of loss and fear of the unknown. Advertising companies have been using fear as their primary marketing and sales tool for many years because they understand that fear motivates decisions.[8] Think of insurance companies selling travel insurance as an example. Most people know that there is an extremely low probability of them becoming ill or injured while on vacation. Nevertheless, people will spend hundreds of dollars more for peace of mind—just in case. Moreover, most people are aware of the concept that a company cannot operate at a loss for an extended period of time, which means that if insurance companies did not earn a significant profit selling travel insurance, they wouldn't offer it. Logically speaking, it is extremely likely that vacationers will not require the use of their previously purchased travel insurance. But many people have such a strong fear of being in a negative situation that they will spend their hard-earned money to prevent such a circumstance. In cases such as these, emotion trumps logic and leads to action.

Utilizing Fear

You can elicit fear from your audience by outlining the negative consequences of a proposed plan of action or a decision. The status quo can also be framed as the enemy here, whereby a lack of decision will result in damage. Highlighting the shortcomings and pitfalls of any situation will cause the audience to think twice before proceeding. The impact of fear is amplified even further if you can connect the fear to audience values such as revenue, optics, stock price, etc. Fear is an even stronger tool if you're able to accurately extend the possible negative impact down to the individual level (i.e., "We can say goodbye to year end bonuses this year"). A quick word to the wise: On most occasions, you'll want to concern your audience, not terrify them. This technique is deceptively powerful, so handle with care.

Back in 2015, Elon Musk was presenting Tesla's newly developed battery technology. At the beginning of his presentation, he showed a large image of a production plant pumping out pollution into the atmosphere. The pollution was so dense that the image showed the sky morphing into a dreary, dark grey color. This visual was a great choice because although Mr. Musk's presentation was based in fact, the visual of the polluted atmosphere is much more powerful than simply explaining the negative impact of pollution on our environment. The image brings the situation to life and is likely to evoke a stronger feeling of concern from the audience, which would benefit his presentation. When people are in a state of concern regarding substantial damage or harm, they are much more inclined to support a safer alternative, potentially overlooking obstacles such as cost, for example.

Hope

Hope is another impactful emotion to persuade your audience during a presentation. Consider implementing this technique when you'd like your audience to stay the course or stand pat in a given situation. In order to evoke the emotion of joyful anticipation, you must A) lead the audience to realize the (sunshine and rainbows) potential positive outcome(s), and B) show the audience that such an outcome is within reach. Presenters can effectively do this by metaphorically painting a picture for the audience of how the best-case result will look. The more detail, the better. Typically, this approach is used near the end of a professional presentation. A highly effective example is when the presenter projects to the audience how their company or organization will compare to their competitors if they make a change, versus if they stay the course (using a particular metric or measurement, such as revenue). When you evoke the emotions of hope and optimism from your audience properly, your audience will become more likely to consider, and therefore agree with your proposal or strategy.

Overall, stimulating a hopeful and optimistic audience is very useful for any presentation. In addition to improving audience reception, it can also have a calming and comforting impact on the presenter themselves. I recommend sprinkling optimistic insights and comments at least in the beginning of your presentation both to engage the audience and to improve the ambiance.

Other Useful Emotional Techniques

Compassion, sympathy, and empathy all have their place in a persuasive presentation as well. The goal in evoking these emotions is to transport your audience to a more understanding frame of mind. This process leads to the audience feeling compelled to become supportive of, and involved in you and your project, respectively. Stories in the form of real-life, firsthand experiences are typically used to achieve this end because they are accessible and relatable. For example, a presenter once told a story about the negative consequences an individual had upon purchasing a particular product. It was a brief, tragic experience that was shared to give a face to the number of customers that had been dissatisfied with the company's latest product. The presenter wanted the audience to understand the real-world impacts of the malfunction, as opposed to focusing on the statistics because she felt that the audience would be more inclined to support her solution. She was correct. By highlighting how the product error can impact an individual, her audience was easily able to envision their loved ones in that position. Keep in mind that using compassion, sympathy, or empathy typically takes some time and, therefore, may not be suitable for your presentation due to time constraints. If you'd like to test this technique out, keep your version of the experience concise at first. Once you have used this technique, you'll have a better understanding of both how to use it, and when it is called for. Crawl before you walk.

Emotional Appeal Phrases and Gambits

- Imagine yourself, or a loved one in **(insert negative circumstances)**
- By making a slight shift in our operations, we could **(insert possible positives)**
- It's truly heartbreaking when **(insert saddening occurrence)**

Logos = Logic & Reason

The final mode of persuasion, logic, is the easiest to understand and the most commonly used mode in professional presentations. The premise is that if the presenter demonstrates evidence and logical reasoning, to their audience, the audience will understand the concept or line of reasoning and accept its value. Logical persuasion relies on the audience having a thought process and value system that aligns with your presentation content. The presenter reveals the facts and information in a methodical, sequential order that will lead the audience to connect the dots and arrive at the same conclusion as proposed by the presenter. For example, imagine a company executive that would like to begin selling their products exclusively online. The executive might consider presenting evidence of similar companies that have made the change to selling exclusively online and realized an increase in profit. A reasonable person seeing this evidence would hypothesize that there would be value in following suit.

Numbers and Statistics

Numbers and statistics to support your persuasive presentation can be compelling evidence. Most people are able to understand and interpret numbers quickly, especially ones that pertain to them. Meaning they can yield much value in a short period of time. However, you'd be wise to space out your use of numbers and figures as a way of providing the audience with time to consider their implications. You might consider following up your figures with premeditated implications that are of value to the audience.

Consistency

This key principle of logic and reasoning as a means of persuasion is based in our faith that the future will behave like the past. I don't make a habit of referencing Dr. Phil, but he does share one sentiment that I have come to agree with: "The best predictor of future behaviour is relevant past behaviour." This principle boils down to tangibly identifying a successful pattern or strategy that has been established somewhere at some point in time, then applying it to the current situation. For example, in the first year of going online, company X realized a 25% increase in revenue. Company Y can then reasonably expect the same or similar revenue increase (assuming, of course, that the companies are in a similar market and industry).

Most presenters in the private sector lean on this mode of persuasion as the backbone of their presentation. It's concrete on its own but you can always combine credibility and/or emotion with logic to enhance its impact. Additionally, you can strategically arrange the order in which to unpack your logical arguments for maximum effect.

Logical Pitfalls

To begin with a warning, presenters have a tendency to pepper the audience with facts and data, which commonly leads to audience confusion and/or disengagement. To avoid this, make sure that you are presenting essential information. Consider explaining why it's essential if you see tilted heads and raised eyebrows. Also, remember to pause periodically so that the audience has time to process the data and information that you've presented.

Another landmine to be mindful of is your audience member's values. They may differ from yours, or what you've anticipated. As a result, your audience may not arrive at the same conclusion as you have, or where you've intended. For example, some presenters are focused on increasing revenue when presenting to their superiors, but at that given moment, public opinion may carry more currency than total revenue, in which case the superiors might not follow your lead. The next landmine to side step is that logic can become boring for the audience quickly. They may be accustomed to hearing facts and information that doesn't directly apply to them. Psychologically speaking, the reason people mind wander or become bored is correlated with a lack of actionable tasks.[9] Meaning that the steady reception of information that is perceived to be of little or no value, leaves people in a dormant state of mind.

So, what can be done? You can make two changes and one supplement. The first change is to strip away any information that is not essential for your audience to know. This will automatically improve the overall effectiveness of your professional presentation as it will be more concise with increased impact. Secondly, you can improve your delivery by explaining to the audience why they should be concerned with specific information throughout your presentation. Take the time to identify how your key content will impact them ahead of time. Then, during the presentation, if you see wandering eyes, emphasize that impact. As a side note, data, facts, figures, and information are always more impactful when accompanied with a visual. Using a clear visual aid can help you to achieve your desired effect.

Logical Phrases and Gambits

- The facts indicate **(insert relevant factual information)**
- The statistics demonstrate that **(insert statistical conclusion)**
- According to the research **(insert relevant factual information)**
- (Stimulant) will cause (response), **which will lead to (result)**

Rebuttal Strategy

The late Stephen Toulmin was a British philosopher of practical arguments and later worked as a professor at many notable universities such as Columbia, Stanford, and USC. One of his greatest accomplishments was his formula for establishing a practical argument. Today it's known as "The Toulmin Model of Argumentation." He researched thousands of proposed arguments during his time and came up with a common formula that the majority of successful arguments share. Since his model of practical argumentation was established in 1958, many of its included elements have been further broken down or expanded upon, such as his use of evidence, claim, etc. Though there is one component of his model that can be integrated into your professional presentations to enhance persuasion: the rebuttal.

The rebuttal is a two-step sequence that bolsters the presenter's position in their persuasion. First, a counter-statement is made that outlines objections (or possible contradictions) to the presenter's position or presentation goal. These can be in the form of one-off exceptions, counter arguments, etc. Secondly, a swift and sound rebuttal or refutation of the counter-statement is stated. For best results, the rebuttal should be cemented in fact.

Rebuttal in Action

Many years ago, I was invited to do some presentation coaching with a non-profit organization. I didn't quite know what I was getting into, but I accepted the invitation because I was just transitioning to professional presentation coaching and was eager to gain more real-world experience. As it turned out, the organization was lobbying a local, municipal government to alter its traffic laws. Their desired outcome was to introduce new legislation that made it illegal for drivers to use their phone while operating a vehicle. Yes, this was long ago... Anyhow, one of the most compelling moments of the presentation was when the presenter stated: "Some people have claimed that using their phones while driving helps them to focus." Then immediately they followed up by stating, "However, the latest research shows that drivers who attempt to use their phone while driving are **three times** more likely to be involved in a **traffic collision**!" The bolded words here were emphasized by the presenter. Though we'll explore this effect more in Chapter Seven (*Vocal Projection*), this rebuttal was very impactful because it resonated quite well with the government officials in the audience.

Persuasive Presentation Structure

The conventional trend for persuasive presentations begins with negative content then transitions to a positive outlook. For example, the presenter might start out by outlining an organization's current problems, challenges, and conflicts, focusing on issues that they plan to address. Then, they elaborate on the potential, subsequent problems if left unresolved. After that, they begin to present the remedy, in all of its glory, by unpacking the positive content that will lead the audience to agree with their solution.

Additionally, there are two sequencing strategies to augment your influence and persuasion. The first is to present your preferred option or direction first. Then, as you present the alternatives, you'll compare it to your initial, preferred option and outline why your choice is superior. Alternatively, you could present your preferred option or strongest point last, then highlight the limitations or drawbacks of the alternative options as you progress through each.

These presenters subscribe to the thinking that "The last impression is the lasting impression." An example of this structure is strongest point-last, next strongest point-first, weakest point(s)-middle. You can think of arranging your points like a relay race team: the anchor is usually the team's fastest runner, then your next fastest begins, etc.

Ultimately, both of the sequencing strategies above are effective. However, you'll need to make a decision at some point. You'll also have a chance to reinforce your strongest point in your conclusion. As a guideline, avoid using more than five main points or sections. Adding main points increases the demand on your audience, which decreases their reception.

Conclusion

The conclusion of your professional presentation will likely be the most memorable part of your presentation for your audience. You should view your conclusion as your last chance to tie all of your content together, and shape the reception of your presentation for your audience. This being the case, the conclusion may be seen as the most valuable part of your presentation.

At this point, you're approaching the finish line, and you may be tempted to replicate Olympic runners, and sprint! However, the contrary is actually more beneficial. Slow down your speaking pace and pause effectively between statements to maximize their impact. Think of this time more as a victory lap. The conclusion of a professional presentation has three distinct purposes:

1. To remind the audience of your most impactful content
2. To remind the audience of why they are there and what their next steps are
3. To close respectfully

You must have a well-organized body in order to close effectively. The framework for a complete and effective conclusion is listed below.

This framework has been specifically designed to include each of the valuable assets in your conclusion, ensuring that you've covered everything, leaving no loose ends.

Professional Conclusion Framework

1. Summarize main take-aways
2. Restate your purpose or next steps for the audience
3. Closing statement and expression of appreciation
4. Invite questions (sometimes)

Visit www.professionalpresentationservices.com to access the free supplementary resources

1. Summarizing Main Take-aways

This component of the conclusion framework is integral in many forms of communication, yet often overlooked. This is your opportunity to paint a final picture for your audience, as you see it, by tying the key information and content together. This component will likely be the longest portion of your conclusion. At this point, you have the opportunity to recap your sections and highlight your main points. Keep in mind that your audience might have forgotten some of the crucial information that you've stated earlier. Also, consider the possibility that some audience members may have misunderstood some key content. This is the time to clarify. Additionally, the audience may have been caught up in peripheral information and bypassed the key content. This is an opportunity to recalibrate their thoughts.

In informative presentations, where presenters are acting as a vessel of communication, simply restate the key content or main points, and possibly offer an interpretation of this content from your perspective. Consider rephrasing your key content and main points to increase the range of understanding by your audience.

For persuasive presentations, continue to summarize key

content and main points. But remember that you may have altered the significance of some of your key content and main points. You may have magnified the main points and key content that are influential in helping you to achieve your goal, and downplayed or glossed over other information that does not directly support your objective. Remember to highlight the right information in your conclusion and you will most likely state your opinion in the form of a recommendation, or proposition.

Listing the main take-aways is meant to create a selective summary of your entire presentation, so don't include everything. You may be tempted to overload this part with content, but please refrain from doing so. To get the most out of your conclusion, start by asking yourself this question: If the audience will forget most of my presentation afterwards, which three or four points do I want them to remember? This question will help guide you in what you choose to reiterate and emphasize in your conclusion. Essentially, recapping the journey of your presentation to the audience, and leading into the next steps.

2. Restating the Purpose or Next Steps

The best professional presentations execute this component of their conclusion in a concise and simple statement. It has a two-pronged effect on the audience. First, it sends a signal to them that you, the presenter, are organized, methodical, and have a well-thought-out purpose. In other words, you are a professional. Secondly, it clarifies to the audience what you'd like them to do next. Even if your purpose is as straightforward as to bring them up to speed on some new policies or procedures that will be instated in the near future, remind them of that. Tell the audience that you wanted to inform them of the latest changes so that they can be mindful of them and act accordingly moving forward, for example.

If you'd like for them to take action on something or change their behavior (i.e., purchase something, invest, subscribe, etc.), then tell them that. Something like, "I'm sure you'll agree that both our current sales numbers and projections paint a promising picture for our company moving forward. We would greatly appreciate your consideration of this investment opportunity. If you decide that you're interested in moving forward, or if you'd like to discuss further, please feel free to contact us (insert phone, email, website, etc.)." The audience will appreciate you clarifying their next steps and will be far more likely to oblige.

Omitting this part of your conclusion may lead to audience confusion. In such presentations many audience members are left thinking: "Do we have to do anything?" or "Okay, what now?" For example, if they were inclined to connect with you and move forward, they may be left questioning how to begin that process. Furthermore, they may be left with a feeling of unease toward the presenter because they have been led astray, which is true to a degree. You could have the most well-organized and structured presentation, but if you fail to direct the audience at the end or at least indicate that there is no action expected from them beyond just understanding, they will likely feel uneasy and confused. You don't want that. You want them to be clear on their role. This is the final opportunity to communicate the meaning of your presentation and stimulate a change in thought or action.

3. Closing Statement and Expressing Appreciation

The formula here is straight forward. Indicate to your audience that your presentation is ending or has come to an end via direct statement. Then, thank them for their time, attention, engagement, and consideration (sometimes). This is another concept that seems simple, yet many unsuccessful presentations overlook. Take three to five seconds to tell the audience that your presentation is now over. This sends a signal to them that they can process and do not need to absorb any more information. It also notifies them that they may have an opportunity to ask a question, so they can shift their brains into reflecting and critical thinking mode.

When thanking the audience and expressing appreciation, you are finishing respectfully and upholding your established, positive rapport. You are also acknowledging their importance and value, which will pay dividends in the future. Your audience will be more positive and less critical of your presentation when asking questions, and they will feel more comfortable approaching you. These positive outcomes are highly valuable for your individual brand.

Closing Statement Phrases

- That brings us to the end of my presentation today. Thank you so much for your attention.
- That concludes my presentation this afternoon. Thank you for being so receptive.

4. Asking for Questions (sometimes)

Although this component of the conclusion will be dependent upon your unique circumstances, it's common practice to open up the floor for questions afterward. Sometimes, you won't have the time, or the situation will not allow for questions. Chapter Nine (*Responding to Questions*) is dedicated to addressing questions during your presentation, but for now you just need to consider using a lead-in phrase.

Closing Statement Leading into Q & A

- We've reached the end of my presentation today. Thank you very much for your time and attention. **If anyone has a question, I'll do my best to answer**.
- That concludes my presentation today. Thank you for being so patient and receptive. **At this point, I'd like to open up the floor for questions**.

Lack of Direction

On a final note, I'd like to share an experience that has always stuck in my mind. On this occasion, I was lecturing to an MBA class on the topic of presentation design and structure. I had previously prepared a video wherein the presenter did not focus on a singular specific topic, but instead went on a series of rants vaguely related to their supposed loose topic. The presenter went on tangent after tangent, as past memories popped into their mind. They seemed to be aimlessly thinking aloud until they were notified that they were out of time and promptly exited the stage. The video was short--only about 8 minutes long--but it served as a tool that I planned to follow-up on by discussing its shortcomings as a class.

I started the discussion by polling the class and asking for a show of hands. "How many of you thought that the presenter was effective?" I asked. Followed by, "How many of you thought that the presenter was ineffective?" I was shocked. Nearly all of the students felt that the presenter was, in fact, effective. I had to explore this further. I asked: "What made this presenter effective?" As it turned out, the majority of students felt that he spoke clearly, passionately, and with conviction. He delivered his content very confidently and used great body language, they reported. All of this was true, but I realized in that moment that I needed to back up a little and refocus my students on the priorities. I asked: "What were the main points of his presentation?" I heard crickets. Then I asked, "What was the topic?" Again, nothing. Finally, I asked, "What do you think his desired outcome was?" As I began to call on students individually, they began to realize that they had no idea what his goal or desired outcome was. So naturally, because we collectively didn't understand what his point was or what effect he intended to have, he was ineffective. The moral of the story is that in order for your professional presentation to have any shot at success, you must outline to the audience what their role is or what their next steps are. If you don't, you've basically led them astray. Follow the professional presentation framework. If you overlook these steps, you are essentially hoping that some positive outcome will arise, instead of facilitating your desired outcome to occur.

Full Conclusion Exemplar

Context: Technology Development Company seeking investment to continue their research into solar energy.

Audience: Venture Capitalist, prospective investors

Conclusion lead-in = *Alright, we're now nearing the end of my presentation.*

Main Take-Aways = *We've reviewed our very promising latest developments in solar energy, our harnessing technology. We've also explored the enormous positive impacts that they will have to businesses, communities, and individuals. Finally, we've detailed our plans to continue to innovate and monetize via establishing a solar energy infrastructure.*

Purpose/ next steps = *We truly appreciate your consideration, and would like to take our company to the next level. If you decide that you're interested in moving forward, or would like to learn more about us, please feel free to reach out to me directly.*

Closing Statement = *That concludes my presentation for today.*

Appreciation Expression = *Thank you so much for your time and attention.*

Ask for Questions = *Does anyone have any questions?*

The Introduction

The beginning of a professional presentation has three distinct purposes:

1. To gain the audience's attention/interest
2. Introduce the topic (get the audience thinking about the topic)
3. Forecast the sections of your presentation to the audience

(inform them of what you'll be presenting and in what order)

When discussing the introduction component within the entire professional presentation structure, it's important to note that not all presentations warrant a full or partial introduction. Some presentations have been successful jumping right into their body content. These presentations have previously established audience interest, topic awareness, and are usually on the shorter side, so there's less of a need to forecast content. Typically, presentations that do not require an introduction are more informal and in-house. Like a project manager presenting to their team, for example. However, when approaching a larger scale or higher stakes presentations, consider reviewing the introduction framework as you'll likely find value given your circumstances. The full scope of an introduction has been laid out for your benefit, and you can feel free to pick and choose as you please for your next presentation. But remember, when you're unsure about your audience or presentation, it's better to err on the side of caution. Go formal.

It's very challenging for any presenter to be successful without effectively accomplishing the three introduction purposes early on in a presentation. Please do not accept this challenge; instead, prepare a couple of lines that will help your audience to engage with you. It can take as little as 20 seconds and make a world of difference. I have provided a concrete framework below as a catchall for any professional presentation to ensure that you have effectively set yourself up for success in your presentation.

Professional Introduction Framework

1. Hook & Greeting
2. Self introduction
3. Topic introduction
4. Roadmap/Overview
5. Purpose

At this stage, if you have trouble populating this framework, you have likely made a mistake or overlooked a body component. Consider troubleshooting.

Visit www.professionalpresentationservices.com to access the free supplementary resources

1. Hook & Greeting

I'm compelled to briefly mention that there are a variety of effective, immediate openings that capture the audience's attention and interest. However, for the purposes of the modern-day professional, we're going to explore the three most effective and practical hooks, and then highlight what to avoid.

Intriguing Question

The first way to open a professional presentation is by posing a question to the audience that's connected to your topic. The question must be relevant to your audience and therefore, will act as a bridge between your topic and their interest. This opening strategy will trigger the audience to reflect on their experiences and existing knowledge in an attempt to address the question. What's more is that audience members have a notable reaction of internal dialogue, such as, "Where are they going with this?" Asking an intriguing question will increase their curiosity and lead to improved attention.

Story Time

A story can be in the form of a past experience, an analogy, a metaphor, etc., but it must be meaningful and connected to both your audience and your topic. Personally, I have found this technique to have the most impact on an audience as many people have been conditioned to increase their focus when they are listening to a story. Hollywood has built a huge industry through this method. If you decide to open with a brief story, ensure that it's no longer than a minute in duration, it takes a twist or turn at the end, and is related to your topic. To begin your story, provide the audience with a time reference and their ears will perk up. For example, "Seven years ago, there was a very small start-up company in the Midwest with very big ambitions." This approach will increase the audience's curiosity and interest as they will become eager to hear both how the story resolves, and why you are taking the time to share it with them. This opening also serves as an excellent segue into yourself and topic introduction.

Once upon a time, I was hired by an Associate Director of a growing start-up company to improve their sales presentations. She informed me that many of the sales team's previous presentations had been recorded, and suggested that I review them. I eagerly agreed as I felt it would be a great starting point. Not to mention, opportunities to view past presentations of current clients didn't happen every day. As I reviewed the footage of their presentations, I noticed that 12 out of 13 sales representatives spent at least 25% of their entire allotted presentation time on their hook. They had designed these complex, suspenseful openings that had the makings of a murder mystery novel. Very intriguing, but they took up far too much time. The presenters were left racing through their precious content, which was intended to persuade the audience to purchase a service subscription. All of that time and effort spent preparing the best way to showcase their service as superior was wasted as they barely skimmed the surface of its advantages. Just as the purpose of your resume is to get you an interview, not a job, the purpose of a hook is to persuade your audience to listen to your presentation, not automatically agree with you.

Shocking or Counterintuitive Fact

The third and final best way to open a professional presentation is with a shocking or little-known fact. This remark will instantly cause the audience to consider whether or not your fact is true. Then subsequently, cause the audience to assess how the fact can be possible and how it impacts their lives. Again, you must ensure that your fact is surprising, relevant to the audience, and connected to your topic. This task can easily be accomplished with a few moments of thought and then a quick Google search. Using a famous quote and then exploring its factuality or modern relevance aloud can also be effective if the information will likely surprise the audience. For example, "I'm sure that many of you would say that you know the difference between one million and one billion. But consider his... one million seconds is equal to 11 and half days. Now what about one billion seconds? One billion seconds is equal to...11,574 days. That's more than 31 years!"

Hook Cautions

Avoid hooks that are too long. Time yourself to make sure that your hook is not longer than a minute. A good hook is about 15 – 45 seconds and arouses the audience's curiosity. Also, avoid plunging straight into content as you risk instantly losing a portion of the audience, and it isn't very likely that they'll come back. Have you ever tried to make sense of a movie starting somewhere in the middle? Not a positive experience. So, make the audience's life as easy as possible and prepare them for what they are about to receive.

Greeting

The greeting can come either before the hook, which would make it the very first words out of your mouth. Or it could come after your hook, before your self introduction. I personally prefer to use my greeting after my hook. However, the difference is negligible either way, so stick to your comfort zone. The formula for a presentation greeting is simply hello + thank you.

2. Self Introduction

If you know your audience and they know you, then you can comfortably skip this step. Many presenters have regular, periodical presentations, such as updates, with the same audience. Therefore, introducing themselves routinely would be almost insulting to the audience. However, if/when you are tasked with presenting to an unfamiliar audience, you should take the 5 to 10 seconds to state your name and job title/position within your organization. If you are presenting to an unfamiliar audience outside of your organization or if your presentation is being recorded for future viewers, you should include your organization name as well. For example: "My name is Michael Jones and I am the Senior Manager of Product Development for Blue Metal Media Inc." Or, "I'm Michael Jones and I'm a Resource Management Specialist. Today, I'm here on behalf of/representing Parent Company Inc."

3. Topic Introduction

Once you have your audience's attention and they know who you are, clarify the topic of your presentation. Your topic is the overarching theme that you are presenting on. In the earlier example of company X wanting to take their service online, the topic would be a new revenue stream or altered business model. This information can be explicitly conveyed in one or two sentences. The degree of formality with which you approach this component of your introduction is entirely predicated on your existing rapport with your audience. So, if you have regular presentations with the same audience, you can be more informal and just mention the topic or you could specify the subtopics in relation to the central topic that your presentation will focus on. For example, imagine your central topic is new battery technology and the subtopic that you will focus on is solar battery technology. You could mention that your presentation on new battery technology will focus on recent developments in solar energy.

In the event that you're addressing your audience for the first time, it's a safe bet to state your topic (what you'll be focusing on in your presentation). Finally, consider mentioning the anticipated duration of your presentation here.

Situations to Avoid

If you immediately begin your presentation with a self introduction and then topic introduction, you risk lulling your audience to sleep or having them reach for their phones. When you begin with, "Hi, everyone: My name is…), you are sending a signal to your audience that they can tune out. Most people have attended so many fruitless presentations that these words act as a trigger to begin mind wandering or spend their precious cognitive energy elsewhere.

4. Roadmap/Overview

Before you launch into the content, information, or arguments of your presentation, you should always give the audience a heads up. The best practice is to clearly outline the overview of your presentation to your audience in the beginning of the presentation and then use signposting language and phrases to keep them on track throughout. At this point, consider accompanying your speaking with a visual agenda. To effectively communicate your agenda or overview in your introduction, you must first have A) determined which content you're going to include, B) grouped or sectioned that content by commonality, and C) arranged or sequenced those sections for your audience.

Basically, you must have the body of your presentation prepared. Next, simply list the main points or section titles that you'll be focusing on in their order of appearance. Illustrating their section title and sequence to the audience is crucial. Stating them explicitly in your introduction will help the audience prepare for the content that you'll be presenting, increasing their ability to follow along with you. It's also beneficial to recap and repeat key points or complex concepts throughout your presentation both to ensure audience understanding and also to recalibrate their attention.

The absence of a forecast or roadmap will leave your audience unaware of what's coming their way. You risk appearing disorganized, as if you're jumping between the content. This caution directly applies to presentations in which multiple events have occurred simultaneously and you intend to inform your audience of these respective situations.

Helpful Hint

Consider pairing your presentation roadmap with specific gestures and body language to improve results. Specifically, count on your fingers when you are listing your sections. This approach will provide your audience with a visual of the roadmap while adding to your confidence.

5. Purpose

In many presentations, both the audience and the presenter will benefit from a clearly stated purpose. From the audience perspective, it builds trust in the form of transparency, and also guides the audience to the desired outcome. Ultimately, sharing the purpose of your presentation with your audience can help them to focus on your messaging. As the presenter, you will also directly benefit from clarifying a home base to connect with your content as you're presenting. Furthermore, it pre-emptively addresses many potential questions. Establishing a home base with your audience assists you in maintaining your focus and keeping your composure. Stating your purpose is most advantageous in informative presentations and more formal presentations. For example, "My goal today is for each of you to have a better understanding of how X works and how it will impact our organization moving forward." For persuasive presentations, you'll want to be selective regarding whether or not to share this information with the audience as it may be counter productive. An example of this would be an executive presenting to their superiors three different options to invest the company's resources. The executive may have their own opinion about how the resources should be allocated and may have structured their presentation to lead the audience to agree with them. However, to explicitly state, "By the end of my presentation today, I'd like you to agree with me, that option three is in our best interest," may not be in your best interest.

Full Introduction Exemplar

Context: Technology Development Company seeking investment to continue their research into solar energy.
Audience: Venture Capitalist, prospective investors

Hook = *In order to power the total sum of our energy needs on Earth, it would take approximately 191 000 square miles in real estate. This area would be dedicated to solar panels harvesting solar energy. That seems like a lot, but compared to the 57 million square miles of land on Earth, that's only 0.3 percent.*

Self intro = *Hello everyone. My name is Joe Roberts, and I'm a co-founder and CEO of New Tech Company.*

Topic intro = *For the next 10 minutes or so, I'm going to be sharing with you some of our most promising and latest developments, as well as our plans to move forward, and change the world.*

Overview = *First, I'm going to explain the recent developments that we've made in solar power harvesting technology. Then, I'll move on to its implications on domestic and international energy consumption. Finally, I'll outline our plans to advance the technology a step further and establish a preliminary solar power infrastructure.*

Purpose = *By the end of my presentation today, I hope that you'll have a better understanding of what we're working towards, at New Tech Company. And that you'll join us in our mission to supply clean energy to the masses.*

Chapter Six

Visual Aid Considerations

In modern, professional presentations it's customary to have visual aids accompany your presentation. Some people refer to these as "slides" or "a slide deck," others refer to them as charts, graphs, etc. Basically, they are all visual aids and typically they're organized using one of the industry standard programs, such as PowerPoint, Prezi, Google Slides, Keynote, etc. Additionally, showcasing physical props are also a form of visual aids. In the past, Steve Jobs and Sir Jonathon Ive from Apple Inc. have used props brilliantly during their product launch presentations. At a specific point during their presentation, they would walk over to the lectern and pick up their new technology. They were able to showcase both its size (in relationship to themselves), its appearance, and its practicality.

Designing and using effective visual aids can significantly improve the impact of your presentation and your probability of success. Not to mention, the use of these visual aids can contribute to your audience's perception of you as a professional. A unique combination of experience and research has led to an understanding of visual aids, which may surprise you and change the way you view your next professional presentation. More often than not, visual aids damage presentations by either being misused or overused.

Advantages of Visual Aids

Visual aids, as their name suggests, are meant to do just that: aid your presentation by providing a visual of the content. First, visuals can assist you in explaining complex concepts and illustrating data or information. Secondly, they can help the audience to understand and interpret your content. Finally, visuals can help to keep your audience focused and engaged throughout your presentation. Overview slides and buffer slides can be used to forecast presentation content and help the audience stay on track. You might also consider integrating visuals between presentation sections, for longer presentations (more than 30 minutes).

Therefore, your task is to carefully select the content and material that would benefit from a visual aid and integrate it into your presentation structure. You may end up with a 30-minute presentation that only requires six slides. This is totally acceptable, even preferable, in certain circumstances. It's possible that much of your content can be easily explained by you orally, or perhaps you'd like to spend more than a few minutes dissecting each visual aid with the audience. It's less likely that you'll have 30 visuals in a five-minute presentation, but the main message here is that there is no magic ratio of time to visuals. It truly does depend on your unique situation.

Process for Incorporating Visual Aids

1. Review your structured content
2. Identify which content could benefit from a visual
3. Select or create a visual to help the audience to understand that concept
   a. Utilize design principles
4. Proceed to the next content

Warning Visual Dependency

Visual aids are intended to support your presentation, not supplant your presentation. In other words, you as the presenter are expected to be the focal point of your professional presentation. Avoid dumping all of your content on slides as this process is not a visual aid. In fact, it's the opposite: a visual hindrance or distraction. Many failures have resulted from listing too much information on slides.[1] Listing all of your information on your visuals is not evidence that you are prepared. On the contrary, it's a signal to the audience that you were either unsure which content to include, so you included everything, or that you didn't care enough to thoughtfully select visuals to support your presentation. Neither of these opinions are favorable to you. So, please resist the temptation to overload your slides with content. Avoid using your slides as a crutch. That's what your notes are for.

Additionally, when you use your visual aids to list information, you signal to your audience that you want them to read. Surprise, surprise, people do not attend a presentation to read; they attend to watch and listen. Then there are some presenters who have made the unfortunate mistake of trying to orally explain a concept while showing text for the audience to read. This method of double communication input results in little to no information being absorbed by the audience, as the vast majority of people cannot read and listen simultaneously. So, make sure that your visuals aids are, in fact, visuals. Limit your text and, if you must list content on your visuals, give your audience a chance to review it prior to addressing it. The rule of thumb for listing content on visual aids is between three to five items. The bottom line is: if you want your audience to read your content, send them a report or memo.

Technical Difficulties

Beware of technical malfunctions. I have seen technology fail on more than one occasion. Projectors overheat, systems or equipment have compatibility issues, batteries die, files are unable to open, and there is always disruption in power or internet connection to consider. It's a fairly safe bet that the provided technology will hold up during your presentation, but it's good practice to think about how you would present your material and content should disaster strike. Sometimes, your presentation may be recessed or postponed under these circumstances, but that will be out of your control as well. You don't want to be left standing in front of a waiting audience, growing impatient as you try to explain to them that your content is on your slides. Consider giving some thought to how you would unpack content and explain concepts to an audience without visual aids. How would your word choice change? What body language would you use to assist your presentation? Because Broadway had it right: The show must go on!

Guiding Principles of Slide Design

You should begin to create visual aids after you have selected your content and structured it according to your audience and desired outcome. The best presentations pair specific content with specific visual aids to clarify and convey meaning to the audience. To accomplish this, simply review your structure and your content point by point. At each point, ask yourself: Would my audience benefit from a visual of this content? If the answer is yes, begin to design your slides adhering to the upcoming principles. But be careful because the follow-up question is: How much will it help? Each visual has a cost.

The cost is time and effort. Not so much your time and effort in creating them, although that is also a worthwhile consideration, but the cost of your audience's attention and cognitive energy. People have limited cognitive energy and focus in one sitting. When you're asking them to continually switch gears and focus on different stimuli, you begin taxing them mentally and risk wearing them out. So, use visual aids to supplement your presentation when you determine that the benefits outweigh the cost. Also, it's not uncommon for presenters to get carried away developing and modifying their visual aids. Be careful though, eventually you'll reach the point of diminishing returns and your time would be better served rehearsing, as opposed to changing fonts for a fifth time.

Principles of Visual Aids

When you create your visual aids, you should be focusing on three distinct principles:

1. Purpose
2. Clarity
3. Cleanliness

1. Purpose – How/what will the visual aid help the audience to understand?

Every visual aid should be specifically designed to assist the audience in understanding. Their purpose will either be to help explain a concept, to prove a theory or trend, or to recalibrate the audience's thought process (get them thinking). When you're creating your slides to accompany your content or points, make sure that you know exactly what the point is that you'd like to illustrate. Then, decide which type of visual aid (i.e., image, graph, chart, diagram, bulleted text, etc.) would best help the audience to understand or agree. For example, many successful presentations include an overview or agenda slide near the beginning. This slide helps the audience follow along by acting as a roadmap of what's to come.

When you begin creating slides without a specific purpose in mind, you immediately risk overloading your slides with unnecessary content. You are essentially asking and expecting the audience to parse out the meaningful content on the fly, which will lead to audience exhaustion, then disengagement.

2. Clarity – Will the audience struggle to understand the main point of this visual aid?

Visual aids and slides should be clear to see and understand. The most common mistake that presenters make is choosing background and font colours that do not contrast well enough for the audience to see. This issue causes the audience to strain and struggle as they try to interpret the visual. To avoid this ordeal, use a system such as "color explorer" or simply Google search "color matching" to select colors that will enhance and not detract from your presentation. Don't make the audience work; do the work for them.

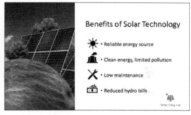

Grouping of visuals or text on a slide is also important to consider as "the law of proximity" specifies that people tend to associate visuals which are close together.[2,3] Groupings can be separated by a space double the width of the grouped text or visuals. Labels are also a worthwhile consideration when comparing multiple visuals at once. Using animations to control the revealing of content can also be useful in helping the audience to follow along.[4]

Furthermore, there is a size relationship that is evident on every visual aid. Size indicates importance of information, so larger images or details within your visual aid are perceived by your audience to be more important than their smaller counterparts. Be mindful of this size hierarchy.

 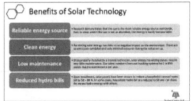

In North America, most people are trained to scan for information from top left to bottom right, so be mindful of this tendency when you're designing. For example, slides that include both visuals and text benefit from placing the visuals on the left and text on the right, to aid the audience's flow of interpretation. And choose a font style or typeface that's easy to read (ie. Georgia or Verdana). Avoid calligraphy.

3. Cleanliness – Is everything on this slide necessary? Can anything be removed while maintaining the meaning or purpose?

The best slides are clean and simple. They accomplish their mission and are professional. They are not cluttered with unnecessary information or design. Quite the opposite, they include more space, and carefully selected visuals to increase the audience's understanding. When using charts and graphs, reduce the number of variables for best results. For example, if you are comparing growth across one geographical area over time, be careful to not include multiple geographical areas. Use more graphs if needed to avoid taxing your audience's focus and cognitive energy. Less is more, and clean is the goal. So, remove any unnecessary bells and whistles.

When using text-driven slides, use point form (bullets) as opposed to full sentences. Remember that you'll be orally elaborating on each point that you display, so you don't need to include every detail. The *newspaper headline* approach, which uses strictly nouns, adjectives, and verbs is a good strategy. Aim to have each message on one line to make the audience's life easier. They'll appreciate your effort and planning. As a final touch, you might consider using the "transitions" and "animations" features on your preferred presentation program to control the timing and display. This movement will serve you well as a prompt, while helping the audience to focus on your point.

The research demonstrates that humans can process up to six items almost instantly, without resorting to counting. At seven or more items, our brains shift into counting mode, which slows our cognitive processing by approximately 500%.[5] Additionally, supplementary research supports *four* as being the magical number in lists.[6] So, aim to keep your total slide items to a maximum of six and lists of content to four.

On a side note, some organizations insist on using their templates when presenters prepare their visual aids. This consistency will limit the selection of color schemes and backgrounds. However, should you find yourself in this situation, you'll still be able to select the appropriate amount of content per slide and organize it for optimal reception. A number of stock phrases to effectively introduce and explain your visual aids are listed below.

Visual Aids Phrases and Gambits

- I'd like to show you... **(name of visual aid)**
- This next visual will demonstrate... **(trend/pattern)**
- This graph/chart outlines... **(trend/pattern)**
- I'd like to draw your focus/attention to... **(specific feature)**
- The highlighted column/text indicates... **(specific feature)**
- This visual represents... **(interpretation)**

Slide Happy Syndrome

Most presentations do not require a seemingly endless reel of visuals. I can't tell you how many times I've been observing or evaluating a presentation and right at the beginning I see the slide counter at the bottom corner of the screen: "Slide 1 of 237." I think to myself, "Here we go..." I have observed and evaluated more than a thousand professional presentations, and I have never seen a need for that number of slides. Yet some presenters have a tendency to go "slide happy." As I was observing these presentations, I found that many slides are glossed over very quickly by the presenter and are not fully explained. Each of these presentations attempted to jam 12 hours of content into a 30 – 40 minute window. After the fifth or sixth presentation that I observed with over 200 slides, I began to approach and ask the presenters why they decided to use that many slides. The most popular response is: "It's good information, and I want people to know about it." One brave MBA student followed up by saying that he wanted to showcase how much market research he had done. I thanked him for being honest, then reminded him that his desired outcome was not to showcase his work ethic. It was to inform his audience of the most promising time, place, price point, etc., to launch their next product. I could almost hear the winning "ding, ding, ding" sound go off as his eyebrows raised and his chin elevated. I reminded him to focus on presenting the audience with the information that they need to help them in their roles, and that his efforts will be recognized through the process. If you focus on showcasing your efforts, your audience is inclined to become bored, frustrated, or both. Not to mention you'll have exposed your intentions of being praised. As opposed to contributing to your organization's success, which damages your reputation and brand.

After over a decade of experience and research on the use of visual aids, here's what I've found: Slide happy presenters have usually spent a minimum of 50 hours learning, understanding, and interpreting their content. They are immersed in their content and have found seemingly infinite, significant information. When they are designing their presentation, they fail to prioritize the most meaningful content while keeping in mind their audience, logistics, and desired outcome. Instead, they tend to view all of their content as "high value content". They then offload their content onto slides, and disregard any time constraints. Needless to say, you'd be wise to avoid this problematic strategy.

Slide Happy Test

Fortunately, there is a simple test to determine whether or not you have put too much information on your slides. No one else should be able to deliver your presentation simply by looking at your slides. If they can, then you've included too much information and content on your visuals. If you've followed the framework, you've done the research, you have acquired the knowledge, you have customized and prepared the content for the audience. You are the EXPERT. Even if you feel like you're not, or you think the audience may know more than you, you are the expert, and you are presenting the information that you deem most relevant.

Slide Design Advice

- Use a title slide that include a neutral title connected to your topic, along with your name and date
- Use a margin around the border of your slides, no text or visuals should be touching the edges

Slides Including Text

- Avoid using more than two different font styles or typefaces
- Choose fonts that are easy to read
- Match fonts or typeface to the theme (i.e., Don't use an old-style font for new tech)
- Avoid listing more than five items on one slide
- Be aware of the size hierarchy, like a webpage, large font and visuals indicate importance
- Avoid using "All Caps"
- Avoid justifying your text
- Use bullets and point form instead of sentences
- Review your slides for spelling and grammar errors prior to your presentation

Slides Including Visuals

- When using visuals to accompany text, place visuals on the left of the slide
- Use more slides with less content
- Each slide should focus on one single message
- Make sure that your font contrasts well with your background
- Avoid using visuals as filler; use them to assist you in illustrating your content

- Limit decoration to enhance meaning and focus
- Design your slides from top left to bottom right
- Use icons and symbols where possible to aid understanding
- Limit the factors and variables in one graph or chart
- Avoid using legends for visuals where possible
- Pie charts should contain between three to six wedges
- Review the order of your slides before you finalize

Slide Advice During Presentation

- Avoid constantly reading from your slides
- Avoid lingering: Show visual, discuss visual, move on
- You will eventually reach the point of diminishing returns; know when to stop and reallocate your efforts

One Slide Deck Fits All

Over the years, I've had my slides requested many times. I recall an experience that I had once as a College Professor and Curriculum Developer. A former colleague of mine, then Dean, had dropped in and attended one of my lectures unbeknownst to me. I had found out later that she had been passing by my lecture hall, heard me speaking, and decided to stop in. There were approximately 400 graduate students in attendance, so her presence went unnoticed. She reached out to me the next day, informed me that she really enjoyed my lecture, and asked if I wouldn't mind sharing my slides with her. I agreed to send her my visual aids, but I noted that they were customized for myself. She responded by thanking me and by assuring that she understood.

"Everyone has their own flavor," she said.

I sent her my visual aids for the lecture, and like clockwork, she emailed me right back.

"Ryan, I'm noticing now that your slides are focused more on key concepts. But I recall you expanding on some content in specific detail, that isn't listed here. Is this everything?" By this time, I knew what she was looking for. She wanted a turnkey slide deck that almost any lecturer could present.

I responded: "Yes and no. Perhaps we could arrange a meeting? I'll be happy to elaborate."

A few days later, we met, exchanged pleasantries, and I began to explain to her my process of creating presentations. I told her that I review all of the content, then select the key content, then organize that content. Basically, following the framework in this guide. I explained to her that I review my content and decide which elements would benefit from a visual aid and how to present that visual aid. I emphasized that the presentation notes are included only when I anticipate a concept being rather difficult to explain. I'll typically include other examples, models, analogies, etc., but only for the more complex concepts. The remainder of the concepts I'm confident to expand on freely because I know what I know, and I know which content I might need a reminder for.

She then asked me, "Are you saying that you can design brilliant visual aids for your own presentations, but not for others?"

I paused for a moment and organized my thoughts in my head. I then began to think aloud saying, "I can, but to be effective, I would need to be familiar with the presenter, less so their content."

I paused again, then followed up with: "Because if I assume that the presenter needs a visual for everything, and create visuals for all of the content, the presenter will A) never get through them all, and B) overload the audience. However, if I knew their strengths and comfort..."

She then raised her hand as if signalling me that she'd heard enough. She exhaled quietly and sharply through her nose, and looked downward towards the floor.

She said to me calmly: "Thank you for your time."

As you can imagine, I felt I had let her down. I remember feeling really down and I spent the entire next day thinking of ways to help. The day after that, just after I arrived at work, I received an email inviting me to a "Presentation Design Seminar Meeting" from the Dean. I had never heard of such a meeting before, but was very intrigued. Later that day, as I approached the meeting room, I was able to see two people through the glass door: The Dean and the Vice President of Academic Affairs. I recall instantly feeling nervous and caught off-guard.

They asked me to take a seat, and then the Vice President of Academic Affairs said: "I hear that you're able to improve other faculty members' lectures and presentations if you get to know them and their course material. Is that right?"

I remember nodding, swallowing, and mustering a trailing, "Yes."

She then asked, "Would you like to?" And the rest is history.

I began organizing and facilitating *Slide Design* and *Presentation Design* professional development seminars for college faculty.

The moral of the story is that presentations should be built around the presenter, not the visual aids. Turnkey or "plug and play" presentation slide decks often fail because they are too generalized. It's far superior to customize slides around the presenter, then to try to adapt the presenter to generic, overloaded slides. The presenter is expected to bring value independently and be the focal point.

Chapter Seven

Vocal Projection

When coaching and practicing delivery techniques with my clients, I always ask them to think about a successful presentation that they've observed, or to envision what they consider to be a highly skilled speaker. I then ask them: What makes that presenter or speaker effective? My agenda here is to get the client thinking about the characteristics of effective speakers, and for them to realize that there are more than one characteristic or attribute. Yet, the default response that I typically receive is either "clear" or "loud." I will wait for a few more seconds to see if there are any other qualities that they can identify. But most of the time, that's it. This response pattern has also been constantly reinforced in my lecturing and training. My follow-up question is usually something to the effect of: "Alright, so you're telling me that if a presenter is clear when they speak and loud enough for all to hear, their delivery will be effective?" This inquiry will cause them to pause and reflect. At this point, I can almost see their gears turning as they're trying to identify the other important elements of effective speaking. I usually cut in on their thinking after a few seconds and say: "Okay, perfect! You realize that there *are* other speaking techniques that excellent presenters use to improve their delivery. Let me show you what they are and how they work." I just need them to become aware that there is more to effective speaking than just using a microphone and articulating each word. Then, they are ready to learn and understand the tools of the trade.

Understanding Your Voice

One of the most beautiful aspects of a professional presentation is the speaking. It can also be terrifying, but once you get through the initial horror (let's call it "discomfort"), you will be able to speak more confidently. Delivering a professional presentation enables you to manipulate your voice, altering the impact and meaning that your words have. Speaking allows you to do so much more than writing does, especially in terms of conveying tone of voice, and clarifying information. The truth of the matter is that when we write text and then send it to someone, we are limited in influencing how the reader will interpret our message. I'm sure that many of you have had the experience whereby some sort of miscommunication has resulted from an email chain or messaging system that had gone off the rails. But for those of you fortunate enough to have avoided this situation, let's take the two-word phrase, "no way," for a spin. This phrase can have many meanings and interpretations based on the context and the frame of mind the reader is in when they receive it. It could be taken as assertive with conviction, it could be taken as disbelief, or it could be taken as surprise or shock. Presenting enables the speaker to shape their messages more precisely so that they are received by the audience as intended. This is where paralinguistics come into play.

Controlling Your Voice

Paralinguistics can be described as a system of methods that alter or manipulate your voice to inform meaning. For our purposes, we rely on paralinguistics to improve audience reception and attention. There are four basic manipulations of voice (vocal tools) through which you can customize your message to your audience. They are:

- **Pace** – the speed of your speaking
- **Intonation & Inflection** – The rising or falling pitch of your voice
- **Volume** – The loudness of your voice
- **Stress** – The emphasis placed on a particular word or phrase

Each of these elements impacts the meaning of a spoken statement or phrase. Together, they can create a tone or emotion of speech. They are highly effective. In fact, humans have become exceptionally good at determining the meaning of oral communication through tone of voice, more than their words. A telephone communications study revealed that tone of voice accounted for 86% of meaningful communication, while a mere 14% was attributed to the words themselves.[1]

To understand the impact of manipulating your vocal elements, compare them to writing. Think about the last email or memo that you've read. Think about the text (all of the words, sentences, and paragraphs). Now imagine that a few words are bolded, a few words are underlined, and a few words are italicized, see the example below.

Excerpt from Thoughtco.com (2020)

We'd like to review some of the **changes** in the new monthly sales *reporting system* that we discussed at Monday's meeting. First of all, we'd once again like to stress that this new system will **save you time** when reporting <u>future</u> sales. We understand that you have concerns about the amount of time that will be *initially* required for inputting your client data. Despite this *initial* effort, we are confident that you will all soon enjoy the **benefits** of this *new system*.[2]

Most people's eyes are immediately drawn to changes in font as they read. In business writing, it is understood that bolding a term implies importance, while italics imply a minor detail or extra information. Manipulating the four vocal elements when speaking have the same effect; they can be utilized to send a signal to an audience and shape the meaning of the words that they are about to hear.

Pace

The first way that you can control or manipulate your voice when speaking is by changing the pace of your speech. You are able to increase and decrease the rate of words that you speak. The average person speaks between 120 – 140 words per minute (wpm). The average person can also listen to and understand approximately 400 wpm. As you can imagine, this leaves quite the gap in communication processing. As a result, many listeners end up mind-wandering to fill the processing gap. So, how can we maintain our audience's attention throughout our presentation? How can we prevent our audience from mind-wandering and encourage them to focus on our presentation? The answer is actually: you can't. Mind-wandering is unavoidable during a presentation or any speaking engagement for that matter. But what you can do is influence what audience members mind-wander about.

You want your audience to be mind-wandering about our presentation and content. You don't want them to be questioning what you've said, but rather to look forward and try to anticipate what you'll say next. You want to arouse their curiosity so that they are eager to learn your interpretations or proposed solutions. You want them to be thinking about how your content fits into their current understanding and how it will impact them. This form of indirect engagement is what leads presenters to use the terms such as, "captivate" or "I had them" when describing their experience with an audience. Let's outline the speaking framework that will steer the audience's mind-wandering in your favor.

The best approach is to first identify three rates of speaking prior to your presentation. The rates of speaking being fast or quick, medium or regular, and slow. Next, you must become self-aware and recognize our individual speaking pace. This rate of speaking will be used as a baseline for your medium presentation voice. If you're having trouble identifying your individual speaking pace, think of your conversational speaking voice that you would use naturally when speaking with a new colleague. Your fast speaking voice would be your voice when you're very excited and can't wait to share some big news with someone, or under urgent circumstances. Your slow speaking voice would be when you're trying to explain a concept to someone and ensure their comprehension.

Increasing the rate of speaking typically sends a message to the audience of either urgency or minor details. In other words, the quicker the pace, the less important the information. Decreasing the rate of speaking typically signals to the audience important information. Begin by establishing these three speeds, and focusing on where and when in your presentation you should alter your pace to improve the meaning. You'll find that once you do this, you'll be able to have more control over your voice and identify which type of speed elicits specific reactions from the audience. Caution: If you sustain a high pace of speaking, you may appear excited, anxious, or nervous. If you sustain a slow pace of speaking, you may appear unprepared, unconfident, or insincere.

The Importance of Pausing

I would be remiss if I didn't share one of the best kept secrets of professional speaking: integrating pauses. Pauses have multiple positive effects on the audience and on your presentation as a whole. For example, when you pause prior to revealing some key information, you elicit anticipation and focus from the audience. When you pause after you deliver a key piece of content, you signal a moment of reflection and consideration from the audience. And when you pause throughout your presentation, you give the audience a chance to recalibrate and refocus their attention. First, you should plan your pauses ahead of time to increase their impact. Once you see the results and the reaction from your audience, this process will come more naturally.

Another pearl of wisdom is to practice replacing hesitation sounds (i.e., Um, ah, uh, etc.) with intentional pauses. Hesitation sounds signal to the audience that you are dividing your focus between thinking and speaking, or attempting to revise your message while you're speaking. Think of these hesitation sounds as the loading or buffering spinning wheel on your computer screen in the midst of streaming a video. There's a collective sense of frustration. Most of us would prefer to wait a moment or two prior to playing the video to ensure its quality. Rather than viewing a choppy poor-quality video to completion. Pause when necessary to reorganize your thoughts, then deliver your content. This technique also pays dividends when addressing questions (Chapter Nine, *Responding to Questions*).

Intonation and Inflection

This is the rising and falling of the pitch in your voice. You can manipulate the inflection of individual words or whole phrases when you're speaking to signal a variety of tones or emotions. When you pair intonation with specific content, it's like installing a guiding system on a missile; much more effective at hitting the target. Consider the following sound that we sometimes make: "ah." Depending on the intonation, it could signal confusion, disbelief, understanding, relaxation, or disappointment. We can manipulate the intonation of any word when we are speaking to alter the meaning of the message as a whole. One of the most universal communication signals is upward and downward intonation while ending a sentence or phrase. Upward intonation signals a doubt or question. Downward intonation signals confidence or confirmation. Consider the difference in meaning in the following statements with differing intonation:

Professional Presentation Services is the gold standard in presentation consulting. = Doubt or Question

Professional Presentation Services is the gold standard in presentation consulting. = Confidence or confirmation

Good presentations implement downward intonation. Excellent presentations utilize both.

Volume

Controlling the loudness of your voice is one of the easier techniques in this guide to master. Many of us have consciously controlled our voice on various occasions in our lives for a variety of purposes. You've most likely yelled, whispered, and everything in between. So now the task is to be able to change the volume of your voice on command. First, let's explore the power of volume. Raising your voice while presenting can demonstrate passion or emotion. It can also stimulate the audience and enhance the energy of the presentation. On the other hand, lowering your voice when you're speaking can emphasize the importance of your message. It can also be used to increase the audience's attention and foster interest among its members.

The challenge for many of us is that, in our past, we have likely altered the volume of our voice subconsciously to achieve a desired effect in a situation. For example, you might increase your volume if you saw a child about to spill something on the carpet. Or decrease your volume as you enter a library. When you are presenting, it's advantageous to intentionally alter your volume at predetermined points in your presentation. First, establish a baseline volume, similar to baseline pace above, then you can increase or decrease your volume in relation to your baseline. The best practice is to implement this vocal technique while rehearsing your presentation. Make a note to slightly lower your volume when delivering what you deem to be critical content and slightly raise your volume afterwards to increase the energy and audience reception. The most effective speakers vary the volume of their voice throughout their presentation, thereby enabling them to capture and maintain their audience's attention and illustrate the importance of their main points. Following the steps in this guide will lead you to become a more polished speaker and professional presenter.

Word Stress & Sentence Stress

During your presentation, you should strive to pronounce each word fully and properly. When you reduce syllables or mumble, you cause your audience to struggle to understand. Essentially you would be forcing audience members to exert more mental energy trying to interpret what you're saying while trying to understand the overall content of your presentation. You can make their life easier instantly with effective pronunciation. In addition, you'll likely have specifically targeted words and phrases to emphasize for the audience. These are called "focus" words because they are the key phrases that you would like your audience to focus on. In order to draw attention to these words, you should stress them while speaking.

The best way to stress key words and phrases is by slightly reducing your speaking pace and volume when you come to these words and most importantly, articulate each word effectively. Completely pronounce each "focus" word in order to emphasize its meaning and significance to the audience. By changing the "focus" word in a sentence, you change the signal and the message to the audience. Consider the following two sentences. The bolded words will signify the different "focus" words:

1. In **2017**, the life expectancy of a person living in the U.S.A. was **78.6 years**.[3]
2. In 2017, the life expectancy of a person living in the **U.S.A.** was 78.6 years.[3]

In the first sentence, the presenter is drawing attention to the life expectancy in years, presumably because they are comparing it to an earlier date's life expectancy. In the second sentence, the country is emphasized. In this case, the presenter is signalling a comparison of life expectancy between countries. Changing the "focus" word changes the meaning of the statement. The formula to correctly identify your "focus" words is to first review your script or the statements and phrases that you plan to use in your presentation. Then circle, underline, or highlight the "focus" words in each sentence. Caution: be selective with your "focus" word choice. If you choose too many words to stress or emphasize, it will diminish the overall impact of your presentation.

Vocal Projection Advice

- **Change it up** - Fluctuating each of the vocal elements and techniques throughout your delivery will improve the overall effectiveness of your professional presentation
- **Manage your breathing** - Slowing your breathing and breathing more deeply will allow you to project your voice further and speak more clearly. Begin taking deep breaths 5 – 10 minutes prior to the beginning of your presentation, then continue as you begin to speak
- **Use your greatest instrument** - Speak from your diaphragm (stomach), not from your chest, throat, or nose. Your diaphragm was designed and intended for your breathing and your voice projection. Speaking from your diaphragm is like using an amplifier for your voice
- **Use repetition** - Repeating key content will assist your audience in remembering information afterwards
- **Use questions** - Build in questions to ask the audience (even if they are rhetorical). When people hear a question, it has a similar effect as when they hear their name; they are more likely to become engaged. Use this strategy to regain attention if you notice your audience is drifting
- **Reinforce the meaning** - Periodically, explain to your audience why your content and material matters. This reminder can be used to reengage them as well

Chapter Eight

Body Language

My hypothesis is that those of you reading this book are aware of body language in some capacity. You have likely observed examples of effective and ineffective body language at some point. For presentation purposes, body language is defined as the use of physical actions to convey meaning and content to the audience. In this chapter, I'm going to take a very focused approach to body language. There are many different aspects of body language, but keeping in the framework theme, I've grouped them into four categories: Posture & Movement, Gestures, Eye Contact, Facial Expressions for ease of understanding. This chapter will foreground the important connection between body language and your presentation's success.

Benefits of Body Language

The importance of non-verbal communication or body language has been well documented over the years. William Shakespeare once said, "Everyone gives two speeches at the same time: one that is heard and one that is seen." Then, in the 1970's, Dr. Albert Mehrabian published his famous research study on communication, wherein he found that 55% of all communication is non-verbal or body language.[1] Though the precise ratio of body language's impact has been since contested, its value to communication is irrefutable.[2] Imagine your boss came to visit you in your office and said: "Your latest presentation was very well done," while shaking their head from side to side. Would you think that you actually did well on your latest presentation? In a great many situations, body language trumps spoken communication. What's more is, in the event of a conflict, or as I like to call, a "mixed message," people tend to believe body language over words because it's viewed as a more trustworthy and accurate indication of a person's emotion or intention.

Many beginners are unaware of their body language when they first start their presentations. Typically, beginners focus on getting through all of their presentation's content. Their body language is simply not a priority to them. However, more seasoned presenters understand that body language, like vocal techniques, can be a very powerful tool if utilized correctly. Remember that you can stop speaking, but you cannot stop your body language from communicating. So, let's turn it in our favor.

Body Language Categories

1. Posture & Movement
2. Gestures
3. Eye contact
4. Facial expressions

1. Posture & Movement

Your posture will likely have a strong impact in two areas of your presentation. But before we get into them, we need to understand what posture is. In lay terms, your posture is the form that your body takes when you are standing or sitting. You can think of it as the way that you carry yourself. When most people think of posture, two variations usually come to mind. They are either slouching (characterised by shoulders rolled forward and down, back slightly hunched in a c-shape, neck extended forward, and head tilted down) or upright posture (shoulders back, aligned with spine, back straight, neck straight, head level, feet flat and slightly apart). Of course, these are the two extremes of posture, but the more you improve your posture, the more your delivery and presentation will improve, as well.

Overall Audience Impact

Your posture during a presentation will have an impact on both your audience and yourself. From the perspective of your audience, your posture constantly signals your level of comfort and confidence. The more upright and composed you are, the more confident you appear to your audience. Being perceived by your audience as confident will lead to the audience being more receptive. Your audience will likely interpret your confidence as expertise, which is valuable when presenting. Also, by adjusting your posture periodically, you can influence the audience's engagement and comfort level. For example, if you lean or step toward the audience when delivering key content, your audience will be inclined to mirror you and lean forward, which will improve reception and rapport. Conversely, if you lean backward or step away from the audience while delivering content, they will interpret you as retreating and be less inclined to trust you or engage with you. Furthermore, moving occasionally throughout your presentation will stimulate and signal to your audience that something is changing and they should pay attention. Similar to your smart phone blinking to catch your attention. Whereas delivering your presentation in a stationary position is more likely to have a dormant effect on your audience.

Posture Impact

When delivering a professional presentation, your posture and movement will also have a physiological and psychological impact on yourself. Your posture will most significantly impact your breathing and your diaphragm. Breathing during your presentation is tremendously important, not only for your speaking and body language, but also to control your nerves, which we'll get to in Chapter Ten, *Controlling Nerves & Reducing Anxiety*. But as far as your posture goes, an upright posture enables you to utilize your entire diaphragm, while a slouching or compromised posture minimizes the size of your diaphragm within your torso. Imagine an accordion able to be fully extended versus one that is limited in how far it can expand. So yes, the obvious benefit to upright and correct posture is that you'll be able to speak more clearly and have more control over your speaking. However, a supplemental benefit is that breathing deeply allows you more control of your entire body. This ability will result in a more controlled (often slower) heart rate, more mastery over fine motor functionality, such as hand gestures and, most importantly, clearer thinking. Your mind will be better able to focus on communicating to your audience, choosing better words to express yourself, and having much more control over the delivery of your content. This opportunity will allow you to be less "me" focused and more "you" focused. Instead of thinking, "I hope that I don't forget anything" during your presentation, you're more likely to be thinking, "Is the audience following along with my presentation, or should I explain it another way?" Yes, this recognition begins with correct posture!

Movement Impact

To effectively utilize your movement when presenting, first establish a home base, where you'll be standing at the beginning, and for a majority of your delivery. This approach is similar to establishing a baseline voice in speaking. Then you can move occasionally during your presentation to another location in front of your audience. Try to avoid obstructing your visual aids when you're moving. And most importantly, stand still when delivering a crucial point. Standing firm when delivering important information will give the audience a chance to focus on what you are saying at that point in time and they will become more receptive. One final tip on movement: if you find yourself using a lectern or podium, feel free to move to the right or left of it occasionally to stimulate and establish a connection with the audience. Avoid hiding behind it.

2. Gestures

Typically, gestures involve your hands, but they can also involve additional parts of your upper body. Basically, they are the manipulation of your hands and other body parts into specific shapes to convey meaning. A common example of this relationship is the "thumbs up" gesture that most people interpret to mean good job, good, yes, or another positive meaning. Gestures can involve large manipulations or small manipulations. They can be sustained for a few seconds or flashed for a millisecond. All of these variations of gestures can impact their meaning in different contexts. You can think of gestures like visual aids; they're there to help you convey content and improve your audience members' understanding of information and concepts.

Gestures Impact on Presentations

Ultimately, combining gestures with the content that you are delivering will impact your audience's understanding of your presentation. So, if you pair the right gestures with your speaking at the correct moment, you can improve your audience's understanding of your content by reinforcing your meaning, which, in turn, will benefit your presentation. However, if you avoid using gestures or pair the wrong gesture with your speaking, you risk confusing or misleading the audience. In general, open gestures such as open arms and palms up are considered warm, and signal to the audience that you are trustworthy and comfortable. Closed gestures, such as arms crossed covering your stomach, are considered cold and signal the audience that either you are concealing something or are uncomfortable.

It's best practice to use open gestures as your default setting and avoid closed gestures except to aid you in illustrating a point. Gestures can be used to demonstrate size, speed, shape, location, and progress. They can also be used to convey more specific meaning, such as listing points or information on your fingers, and pointing to your wrist to illustrate time or lateness. When it comes to culturally specific gestures, especially in North America, there are too many to list. Fortunately for us, we use more than we realize throughout our daily lives and many of these gestures will come naturally to you while you're speaking. Much of the time implementing gestures will get ironed out as you rehearse, which leads to the question: How can you get the most out of your gestures?

Using Gestures Most Effectively

Most presenters use gestures either intentionally or unconsciously. The best presenters use a combination of both impromptu and premeditated gestures to enhance the meaning and understanding of their presentation content. Beginners might feel uncomfortable relying on their instincts to naturally produce correct, accompanying gestures throughout their presentation, which is understandable, especially since many presenters do not present routinely. Whatever your comfort level with gestures is, the path to utilizing gestures begins in the delivery rehearsals. During your delivery rehearsals (Chapter Eleven, *Rehearsals, Going Virtual, & Final Send-Off*), you will be practicing delivering your content to the audience. In doing so, you'll find that there are points throughout your presentation that would benefit from emphasis, clarification, or reinforcement. These points are the first that you should look to pair with an appropriate gesture. From there, you will either have one in mind already that you can use, or you may perform a simple Google search for one to adopt. Once you've completed this process, rehearse the specific parts of your presentation that involve gestures. You will refine and become more fluent with their usage. For example, you might count on your fingers to list your presentation's agenda or main points.

Then repeat this process with other key content that you determine gesture worthy. Once you begin this process, you will likely add some impromptu gestures along the way as you become more comfortable using them, which is also beneficial.

Gesture Insight and Advice

- **Show your hands** - Never present with your hands in your pockets, behind your back, or with crossed arms. These gestures signal that you're not comfortable, your hiding something, or that your audience is an afterthought
- **Be aware of the "gesture window"** - which extends vertically from your neck to your waist, and horizontally from about six inches outside of either shoulder. The majority of your gestures should remain inside of this area. Gesture outside of this area too often, and you will appear uncontrolled or erratic to your audience

- **Avoid overusing gestures** - Overloading your presentations with gestures will diminish the impact of your more important gestures and it also may make you appear erratic to the audience
- **Rest your hands** - When you're not gesturing, your hands should be relaxed at your sides. This will register as you appearing calm and composed to your audience
- **"Invisible Watermelon" technique** - When you are explaining a concept, and there isn't an obvious corresponding gesture, consider holding an invisible watermelon in front of your stomach when speaking. This gesture signals that you're speaking about something tangible and significant
- **"Hand Scale" technique** - Elevate your hands to demonstrate growth, decline, or comparison

- **Avoid gesture mismatch** - Make sure that you are using the correct gestures to convey your intended meaning. If you send a mixed message (i.e., Nodding your head while saying "no," you risk confusing your audience
- **Verify correct gestures** - Double check that you are not using offensive or inappropriate gestures during your presentation. This is more prominent when presenting to international or cross-cultural audiences. A gesture that might be common and appropriate in one culture might be inappropriate in another culture. For example, the "A-ok" hand gesture in North America

may be offensive in another culture.

- **Avoid fidgeting at all costs** - Fidgeting is the unconscious movement of your body for an extended period of time. The following gestures would be considered fidgeting:
  - Tapping your fingers
  - Biting your nails
  - Touching your hair
  - Shaking your leg
  - Adjusting your clothes
  - Clicking a pen

3. Eye Contact

Eye contact is the action of looking at another person's eyes to express meaning (consciously or unconsciously). Eye contact is one of the easier concepts to understand, but often a difficult technique to execute. Many of us are exceptional at making eye contact unconsciously in our day-to-day lives, but when it comes to controlling our eye contact in a meaningful way, it can become a daunting task. Eye contact during a professional presentation means routinely looking into different audience members' eyes while you're speaking. One followed by another, and so on. This interaction is meant to be done continuously throughout the majority of your presentation.

Eye Contact's Impact

Making eye contact effectively will dramatically improve your presentation. First of all, making eye contact with each audience member builds a connection between you and them and strengthens your rapport. Furthermore, making eye contact regularly portrays you as honest, sincere, and trustworthy. On top of that, you will appear confident and passionate about your presentation. Effective use of eye contact will also encourage your audience to engage with you and focus on your message. Not to mention, the benefit of being able to read the audience's body language and determine if you should continue on as scripted, or double back and explain your content in another way. Finally, contrary to popular belief, making eye contact with your audience members will help you to remain composed and improve your speaking to meet your audience's needs.

Making Eye Contact Work

Please read this part carefully as you are about to learn the formula for eye contact success. Before you begin speaking, you should choose one person from the audience. The further this person is from you, the better. Look at this individual initially when you begin your presentation. By this point, you should have your opening and introduction pretty well rehearsed, so you shouldn't be focusing on what you're saying, but rather reaching that selected person with your speaking. Once you have delivered your hook and/or self intro, move your gaze off of your initial person to someone quite close to you and state your topic and/or purpose (this will be shorter). Then, move your gaze a third time to someone in the midrange of your audience and explain the overview of your presentation.

This process will bring you to the end of your introduction and the beginning of your body. You will have the ability to pause at this point and scan the entire audience. For the remainder of your presentation, shift your gaze from the right side of the audience to left, alternating between each content point or subpoint. Naturally, you'll be looking at your visual aids while explaining them and you may look up, down, or at your notes occasionally, but the majority of your presentation will be spent looking at the audience. Once you begin the sequence outlined in this chapter, you will find eye contact becomes quite effortless to implement. You'll quickly find that it's not an obstacle to overcome, but another tool to help you.

Reciprocal Eye Contact

Your audience's eye contact, or lack thereof, can be used as an indication of how your presentation is being received. As you gain more experience, you'll be able to read the room and determine if you should change methods or employ an attention-grabbing technique, such as asking a rhetorical question. Changing visuals is also effective in collecting those wandering eyes. However, you should always keep in mind that a lack of eye contact does not necessarily mean that audience members are checked out. They may still be listening or even reflecting on what you've said. When you look out at your audience and you don't see everyone's eyes, you should present to those who are looking at you. Then, when the others look in your direction, you can reconnect with them. This exchange will encourage them to stay locked in throughout the remainder of your presentation.

At the end of the day, you need to keep in mind Plato's ancient words of wisdom: "Everyone that you meet is fighting a battle that you know nothing about". Your audience may not be displeased or bored by your presentation, but rather have heavier, personal issues on their mind. You may be inclined to interpret their body language negatively. Try to avoid taking offense. Instead, accommodate them as much as you can, and stay your focus on the eyes that are on you.

Eye Contact Cautions and Advice

- **Look between the gaps** - The best advice that I can give to you is that if you are nervous about making eye contact initially, focus your gaze on the spaces between individual audience members. This technique will keep your nerves at bay while maintaining a positive impact on your audience. You can also look at their foreheads

- **Avoid staring** - Avoid maintaining eye contact with the same person or people. This constant gaze may make the individual(s) feel uncomfortable. Regularly alternate your gaze (left, right, front, back)

- **Face your audience** - Looking up or down for too long, especially while speaking, signals that you are unsure about your content. Or that you are being disingenuous. Neither are beneficial for you

- **Cultural considerations** - Be aware that cultures view eye contact differently. For example, some of your audience members may purposely avoid eye contact with you as a sign of respect. Keep this fact in mind, and carry on

- **"Preheat" your visuals** - When revealing a new visual aid, do not begin explaining it right away. Instead, give your audience a chance to view it for about two seconds. During this time, watch the audience to determine their level of engagement and understanding. Then either recalibrate, adjust, or proceed accordingly

4. Facial Expressions

Facial expressions involve manipulating the muscles in your face to convey emotion or meaning to your audience. The two facial features that you have the most control over are your mouth and eyebrows. However, there are many muscles in your face that you flex on a daily basis to convey meaning or emotion. As with gestures in our day-to-day lives, we use facial expressions constantly, but are often unaware of them because they are on autopilot, compliments of our subconscious. Facial expressions are among the most recognizable components of body language by your audience.[3]

Facial expressions tell the audience the way you feel about what you're saying. For example, when you make a statement and have a stern and serious facial expression, you signal to the audience that what you've just said should not be taken lightly. Furthermore, your facial expressions will influence the audience's mood as they listen to your words. When you make a statement while smiling, your audience is likely to be in a more positive mood as they interpret it.

Utilizing Our Facial Expressions

By controlling your facial expressions, you'll more effectively maintain the audience's engagement and improve your speaking during your professional presentation. While you're presenting, you're on display and your audience will be observing you. In their mind, they will be unconsciously collecting and interpreting data from your behavior while you present.[4] They'll be watching your entire body, but they will be focusing on your face. Seeing the changes in your facial expression will capture their interest while simultaneously giving life to your words. This complementary technique will improve their attention and they will become more receptive as you deliver your content.

People have been programmed from birth to mirror the facial expressions and body language that they receive. Consider a parent playing with a newborn. Notice that, instinctively, the parent will smile and model the behavior that they would like to see from the child. Smiling is the most powerful facial expression. When you develop a smile in front of the audience, and sustain that smile for a few moments, you'll begin to see the individual audience members smile back at you. We usually raise our eyebrows to convey surprise or understanding. But manipulating your eyebrows can be used in a variety of situations to improve your messaging. Similar to smiling, when someone raises their eyebrows at you, you need to fight the urge to not raise yours right back. Furthermore, when you speak while you're smiling, you will notice that you actually sound happier. Your facial expressions, conscious or not, have been proven to influence your mood and by extension, your tone of voice.[4]

Facial Expression Mismatch

One of the key ingredients in the recipe for presentation failure is facial expression mismatch. This issue occurs when the mood or emotion that you are conveying with your facial expression contradicts your message. In early 2019, I was observing and advising the personnel of a medicinal manufacturing company. Through my process of reviewing and analyzing their product presentations, I noticed this significant issue among a number of the presenters. The trend was that the presenters began their presentation by smiling, then continued to smile throughout their entire presentation—even though their content referred to chronic illness and disease. It was as if they focused on two rules: communicate all of your content and do not stop smiling.

The audience members, in turn, were lost. They were left with puzzled expressions, as if questioning whether the content presented was serious or a joke. As the presenter carried on through their content, the audience members were now forced to use more of their cognitive energy to accurately determine the meaning of each piece of content. The mood had changed to unease and I could see the audience members revert to acting disengaged and passive. This was a clear case of facial expression mismatch but, fortunately, the remedy is tangible. I advised and coached their presentation team to match the mood of their content with their facial expressions prior to their presentation (in the rehearsal stage). And to focus on their audience's reception of the content during their presentation. After a short time, the issue was resolved and their profits began to increase. What's more is the feedback that had been collected afterwards indicated that the company optics had improved in the public eye as well. All of these positive impacts stem from a change in facial expression. The moral of the story: mind your face.

Facial Expression Cautions and Advice

- **Default smile** - The best presenters make their default facial expression a slight smile. This expression will make you appear more friendly on the whole, while allowing you to deviate from your smile to other expressions with more impact
- **Facial awareness** - Be aware of your resting facial expression. Some people tend to appear angry or upset when they are concentrating

- **Avoid expression mismatch** - Correctly match your facial expression with your content when delivering. Avoid sending mixed messages (i.e. smiling when delivering negative information)
- **Perform beta-testing** - Rehearse at least once using a mirror so that you can see what facial expression you are projecting at various points throughout your presentation

Chapter Nine

Responding to Questions

The question and answer portion of a professional presentation can be the most nerve-racking. The perception is that you're no longer in control because the scripted part of your presentation is over. However, questions are actually a good sign that your audience is involved. Before we get too deep into the weeds anticipating the types of questions that you'll be asked, how to prepare for them, and how to respond to them, let's establish the format for responding to questions. The two main ways that questions from your audience can be posed during your presentation is either ongoing throughout your session, or at the very end. I recommend allotting time at the end of your presentation to answer any inquiries. This opportunity will allow you to focus on your delivery during the scripted part of your presentation and not have to worry about being interrupted or side tracked. Often, questions that arise during the middle of the presentation are addressed via the presentation shortly thereafter. The questions, in this case, just serve as speed bumps slowing your momentum and train of thought. Sometimes, your workplace may have a custom or routine established that dictates when questions from audience members will be asked. If you have the option, you should take three to four seconds of your introduction and simply say, "If you have any questions during my presentation, there will be a dedicated Q & A session at the end, and I'll be happy to address them with you then." Or "Please hold any questions for the end of my presentation." These comments are completely acceptable.

Post-Presentation Question Types

There are essentially four types of questions that you could be asked during your professional presentations:

1. Direct Questions
2. Elaboration/Expansion Questions
3. Connection Questions
4. Clarification Questions

Understanding what they are and how they are used will help you to anticipate what you might be asked and to prepare an effective response.

1. Direct Questions

These questions are directly related to the content that you have presented and, in turn, require a concise, direct answer. These questions usually begin with "why" or "what" and target a focused topic. For example: "You mentioned that we are currently selling 12% less product in our northern district than the others. Why is that?" In this example, the question invites a focused response on reasons for the difference in sales.

2. Elaboration/Expansion Questions

These questions request more information on content that was covered in your presentation. These questions usually begin with "can" or "would" and target a more expansive, comprehensive explanation/response. For example: "You've said the market research has indicated that altering our business model will yield more revenue. Can you give us some more detail on that?" In this example, the question asks for more data on the market research, the business model changes, and the projected revenue increase. Basically, the presenter will have to walk the audience through their process to provide them with an understanding (presumably some of this would have been covered in the presentation, so the presenter would briefly review the previously covered component, then address the others).

3. Connection Questions

These questions seek to uncover/determine whether or not there is a connection between the content that you've presented and peripheral content (existing information outside of your presentation). These questions usually begin with "is" or "does" and seek a response pertaining to details of a relationship. For example: "Is there any correlation between our product development timeline and the time of year?" In this example, the question asks if one element is affecting the other. Extending the example, if the new product is a snow blower, you probably don't want to launch it in June.

4. Clarification Questions

These questions seek an alternative explanation of some of your content, or a review of a part of your presentation (usually broken down into sections or stages). These questions typically begin with "can" or "would" and seek an understanding of a previously explained concept or point. For example: "I'm not very clear on how our new partnership with company X will benefit our shareholders in the next quarter. Can you please run through that part again?" In this example, the question asks to review a cause and effect concept from the presentation to improve understanding.

Preparing to Address Questions

When you first begin addressing questions from the audience, you will likely be more inclined to provide them with a response that's palatable. But as you get more experienced, you'll realize that a majority of the questions have a particular structure. When you are able to identify this structure, you will understand more quickly what they are asking, both directly and indirectly, and you'll be able to field questions more favorably.

Remember, you are still in control; you are always steering the ship and, during the Q & A, you are able to steer with your response. Traditionally, after you've responded to at least three questions, you can end your presentation any time and not lose face. This understanding should add some degree of comfort as you engage in your question period. Although you must be mindful of your time.

Responding to Questions Strategies and Advice

Your goal when you're fielding questions at the end of your presentation is multifaceted. Maintaining your professional demeanor and conduct is paramount. When you address concerns in a calm and controlled manner, you signal to the audience that you are prepared and confident. The list of strategies and advice below has been compiled for your benefit. As you read, you'll find your comfort level beginning to rise. Each strategy offers insight into either what to expect or professional methods of responding. These are the tools needed to effectively respond to questions in a professional presentation setting.

- **Use the proximity approach** - If you are in charge of selecting questions from the audience, start with those closest to you in physical proximity and then work your way back. This approach shows that you are mindful of your surroundings, and leads to a more positive perception
- **Buying time** – When listening to a question, you may need time to mentally prepare your response or organize your thoughts. When the question has finished, immediately state: "That's a good question" or "That's interesting." Doing so leads the questioner to feel validated and content, while providing you with time to think and formulate a response. You can pause for a few seconds comfortably, then deliver your response. Remember that our audience is, on average, up to three times (3x) more patient than we are with ourselves[1]
- **Listen to the entire question before you respond** – Inevitably,

you will be asked a predictable question where in the first four words, you can already predict what the question will be and you know how you want to respond. Presenters have a tendency to jump the gun and answer questions before the audience member is finished asking, cutting them off in the process. First, there is the slight possibility that you may be incorrect in your prediction of their question, which will leave you looking over-eager and possibly arrogant (not good). Not to mention that it will put you in a tough spot to continue with their question. Secondly, and more importantly, even if you are right, you've shown that you are impatient and assuming (not good). Instead, listen to the question fully while slightly smiling and nodding. This agreement will show that you are receptive to and interested in understanding them (very good). Then deliver your response. Most presenters have indicated that they jump in on questions to save time. However, it's far more likely that adrenaline and increased nerves play a role in presenter's inclination to respond quickly

- **Repeat the question** – Upon hearing a question, especially in larger venues, it's wise to repeat the question for the entire audience before you respond. This strategy will help the remainder of the audience follow along, while showing that you are considerate of all. This approach will also help you to clarify the question, in case you misunderstood the initial question

- **Rephrase the question** – addressing the question is very important and sends multiple signals to the audience. If someone asks a question that doesn't make sense to you, rephrase or state a similar question to ensure that you are on the same page. You should use a lead-in gambit such as: "Are you asking..." This tactic will not only confirm the question, but also demonstrate to the audience that your concern for them is genuine/authentic. The best part of this strategy is that if your rephrased question is incorrect, the audience member will rephrase it more clearly for you without you having to ask them directly

- **Maintain eye contact** – Focus your gaze on the questioner as you deliver your answer. This conveys sincerity and appreciation for the audience member. You may look down if you need to ponder your response momentarily, but return your gaze to them as you respond

- **Be concise** – Keep your response short while including the desired information. Avoid adding filler info or rambling

- **Mind your word choice** – When responding, use words and terms that the audience will understand. Be careful when using abbreviations or jargon

- **Use analogies and metaphors** – People tend to relate better to explanations in these forms. Prepare a few ahead of time to keep in your back pocket if needed

- **Be positive** – You may be asked a negative question at some point. Someone might criticize your content or presentation of that content in a negative way. The formula for handling negative questions is as follows: First, listen carefully, while nodding. Then, acknowledge their concern and its significance to them (demonstrate empathy). Finally, explain the positive reasons and benefits of your decision or presentation. I have never seen this formula fail. It diffuses the negative situation every time and leaves a positive impression with the entire audience

- **Remember your desired outcome** – During the Q & A component of your presentation, try to keep your desired outcome in the back of your mind. Take the opportunity to reinforce your main points or goals when possible by utilizing response gambits such as: "What's most important here is…" or "Remember the main point is…"

- **Handling off-topic questions** – Every once in a while, you will get a question that's from way out in left field, totally unrelated to anything that you've presented. You will have the natural inclination to respond: "What in the world are you talking about?" or some variation of this. Instead, resist this urge and use this question as an opportunity to reiterate your main message. You can use a gambit such as: "Thank you for your question. I'm actually focusing on X today, but perhaps if we can connect afterwards. I can help to answer that question." This approach maintains your professionalism and fields the question appropriately. Note that you do not have to answer every question, but you should address each question

- **When you don't know** – Eventually, you will be asked a question that is related to your topic but you don't have the answer to. Hopefully, the answer will lie in the excess information and notes that you have on hand (see Chapter Four, *Content Selection*) and you can quickly refer to them. If not, and you still need to respond, honesty is the best policy. First, acknowledge the question, then provide the audience member with direction. An example gambit that you can use is: "That's a great question. Unfortunately, I don't have the answer at my fingertips. But please touch base with me after this presentation and I'll be happy to follow up with you." In this case, of course, you will be expected to connect with them afterwards providing the corresponding information, but this will buy you some time to find and then frame the answer. Keep in mind that you are not expected to know everything, but you are expected to know a great deal and where to find the rest. Avoid saying the words, "I don't know," in isolation

- **Handling prying questions (rumors/secret sauce/etc.)** – When you are faced with a question that you feel uncomfortable answering, because you might be speaking out of turn or not at liberty to say, employ situational honesty. Use a gambit such as: "I think that I understand what you're asking, but unfortunately I can't comment on that. My goal today is to… (reiterate main point/message)" or something similar. Avoid rambling on and divulging any unnecessary information

Presentation Final Closing

Eventually, either your time will run out or your audience will run out of questions. At this point, thank the audience again for their time and attention. Offer them the opportunity to reach out to you afterwards if they still have questions. This invitation reinforces to the audience that you are there to support them, and builds your positive image. Most will never reach out afterwards, but proposing the offer will comfort them and add value to your stock. Then feel free to smile, give a head nod, or a brief wave, then exit the stage maintaining your composure. You might consider seeking a drink of water and a calm area for a few moments in the event that your adrenaline is still pumping. This change of scenery will enable you to gear down and recalibrate. In the event that you are approached by an audience member afterwards, you'll be better equipped to address them.

Chapter Ten

Controlling Nerves & Reducing Anxiety

"There are two types of public speakers... those who are afraid and those who are liars"
– Mark Twain

In the business world, time is money. Many people have busy schedules and busier lives. So, when a presentation is requested from you or required of you, it is likely of some importance. It's safe to say that people are not likely tasked with delivering a presentation as a "make work project" because others are involved, committing their time to observe. When you are required to design and deliver a professional presentation, there's reason behind it. The stakes are high in the world of professional presentations. Oftentimes, financial and career implications are on the line. Your reputation is on the line. Perhaps your idea, plan, or months of your work are on the line. They could be viewed as an excellent investment, or a waste of time and resources. You could be up for promotion, or at risk of being passed over and relegated to menial duties.

Understanding Expectations

Then of course, there are the times when you're not sure exactly what's expected of you or what you're expected to produce. During preliminary meetings with my clients, I will ask a series of questions to get a better picture of their unique scenario and circumstance. Countless times, I've heard the responses, "I don't know," "I'm not sure," or "I think so." I quickly deduced that many business professionals are simply unsure about the presentation process and/ or why they are presenting. In the industry, many are presumed to know how to design and deliver a professional presentation. This misconception is like expecting a mechanic to present effectively on engine configurations. They may be exceptional at repairing vehicles, but professional communication is a whole other animal. They require two completely different skill sets. It's one thing to understand and produce in your role; it's quite another to present content effectively. On top of that pressure, you will be alone, exposed, isolated in front of many people, some of whom are strangers. And let's not forget, you'll only get one shot at success. Sounds appealing, doesn't it? Professional presentations have all the makings of a train wreck.

Yet, in spite of all of the pressures and discomfort, there is hope. In this chapter of the guide, you'll learn about the nature of presentation anxiety and how your nerves can affect you when you are up front. Most importantly, you'll learn what can be done to manage and keep your nerves in check while delivering effectively. The more calm, composed, and comfortable you are, the better you will perform. So, the goal becomes to make yourself as comfortable as possible. Former boxing heavyweight champion, Mike Tyson, once said, "Everybody has a plan until they get punched." This chapter will teach you to prepare for that blow, soften the impact, and then deliver your presentation effectively.

Our Nervous System

Presentation anxiety or nervousness is the physical manifestation of your nervous system overreacting. For many people, this feeling can be more than discomfort. It can be crippling and quickly derail an otherwise well-prepared presentation. However, you need not fear, as the road to anxiety reduction under these circumstances begins with understanding. It stems from the fear of being outnumbered, a derivative of agoraphobia. Its official term is *glossophobia*. This is a very well documented phenomenon that has been prominent for millennia. A few thousand years ago, if you were surrounded by many people that you didn't know very well, or at all, you may have been in danger. Your instinct would have been to remove yourself from the situation as soon as possible.[1] Your focus would have been on the crowd of people confronting you and identifying an exit strategy. Unfortunately, our psyches have not adapted quickly enough to our modern world, and this instinct remains. Our brains release adrenaline into our bloodstream when we are faced with a dangerous situation. This prompts a response to fight, flight, or freeze. Our body's physical reaction result in:

- Rapid, shallow breathing
- Increased sweating
- Loss of focus
- Dry mouth
- Blurred vision
- Cold hands and feet
- Avoiding eye contact

When this occurs, our minds are jumping from thought to thought quickly, consuming huge amounts of cognitive energy. Our thoughts are flipping back and forth between presenting our content and searching for threats. Often, this dilemma leaves the presenter stumbling through their presentation as they constantly try to maintain their focus. Some presenters resort to racing through their presentation to finish as quickly as possible. If you have ever experienced this ordeal, you are human, and you are normal.

The most common presentation fear is that your audience will judge negatively. Many presenters are concerned that they will appear foolish, unprepared, or unprofessional. Others fear that they will forget to mention key content and information. And some are afraid that they will be put on the spot with a question that they won't know the answer to. These are all plausible outcomes unfortunately, and telling you that "it'll be okay" or "you'll be fine" is simply not going to help you. I'm going to share with you some of the most practical and successful strategies to reduce your presentation anxiety and control your nerves. Utilizing these strategies will increase your comfort level when presenting, and by extension, your success rate.

Developing Confidence

It's no secret that the best public speakers and presenters are confident. However, that is not to say that you cannot deliver a successful professional presentation if you are nervous. I have observed many, very frightened presenters that have been successful. Remember that we define success as achieving your desired outcome(s). The difference between the successful and unsuccessful presenter is not the quality of their speaking, but the value of their content. Although we must acknowledge that the more you increase your confidence, the more you increase your probability of success. Think about any activity in your life. Chances are, if you do it confidently, you'll be more effective. There are two paths to improve your presentation confidence. The first is through *preparation* and the second is through *exposure*.

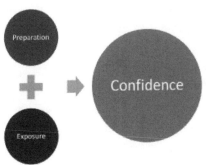

Preparation

Professional presentation preparation means becoming very familiar with your content and material. You should aim to know approximately three times (3x) more information and details than your audience. Earlier in this guide, I referred to the presenter as an expert because when you are presenting on a specific topic, it is presumed by the audience that you have specialized knowledge to share with them. Why would they be listening to you otherwise? You will be providing them with new information or a new concept that they are previously unaware of. The path to becoming more confident presenting in front of an audience begins with having a firm grasp on your presentation material and content. You'll then develop more confidence because you will have organized your content in a clear and logical structure. Your confidence will increase further because you will have developed visual aids to assist you in explaining the more complex content. Essentially, you will have made yourself an expert on the topic and will have prepared your presentation in an audience-friendly manner.

Rehearsal is also key in preparation. Rehearse your presentation aloud as often as possible prior to your presentation date. You can do this in front of a mirror to observe your body language. You can record yourself and listen to your vocal projection. You can rehearse in your bed before you go to sleep at night. Just keep rehearsing as many times as you can prior to your presentation. This practice will help you iron out any issues such as word choice or organization, and will also develop muscle memory for your presentation. When your presentation time comes, the words will come to you like a reflex. Like the lyrics of your favourite song, you'll find that you will pronounce them just like you've rehearsed earlier. You will likely also have the advantage of using visual aids and you can use them to regain your focus and composure, if needed. Basically, if you follow the framework in this guide in advance of your upcoming presentation, you need not fear overlooking key content or appearing unprofessional. The Boy Scouts had it right: "Be prepared."

Exposure

Unlike preparation, you can only gain exposure by speaking in front of others. The basis of this remedy has been well established in psychology for a number of years. If a situation makes you feel uncomfortable, the longer that you can endure being in that situation, the more comfortable you will become.[2] The problem is, it's human nature to avoid uncomfortable situations, and then to remain uncomfortable. For the purposes of developing confidence, consider taking progressive steps toward lessening that fear and anxiety.

The first step is to speak as much as possible while standing. Make an effort to stand up when you speak. You may not want to do this at work if you're asking a colleague for an office supply, as if you're making an announcement. But, when appropriate, make an effort to speak while standing up. This effort will make you feel more comfortable while delivering your presentation. Secondly, you should visit your presentation venue (if possible) ahead of time, and take your place. It would be optimal if you could rehearse in the same venue, but in any case, standing while speaking and scoping out your future presentation venue will help you to anticipate your experience. This exposure will lead to lower anxiety and increased confidence when you deliver your presentation. It's also worthwhile to have a seat where an audience member would, to gain their perspective, but the main idea here is to gain a visual expectation.

Brave New World

Fortunately, due to advances in technology, there are now virtual reality programs and apps available for your benefit. They range in quality of reality simulation and price, but this virtually simulated presentation experience is second only to the real thing. Some of these programs are available on your phone, whereas others require that you purchase particular hardware. For the most part, they all will make you appear to be sporting night vision goggles, but to your eyes, you will appear onstage in front of an audience. You can then practice delivering your presentation while attempting to make eye contact and read the audience. This method will also prepare you for your big day by familiarizing you to the sensation of being isolated in front of a group.

Presentation Dynamic Fallacy

The macro strategy and hack to becoming more comfortable when you're presenting is to change your mindset in how you perceive the audience. As humans, we are programmed to view our audience as our enemy. A sort of "them versus me" dynamic is created in our minds. We think that they are going to pick at and criticize our presentation every chance they get. We believe that they are going to try to trip us up with a question or behave disruptively to throw us off. I envision many of you reading this and nodding while at the same time realizing that this belief is faulty. You are correct. The truth of the matter is that your audience is not your enemy; they are your teammates. You are all in the same boat, you're just the captain. Recall that the dynamic is actually "presenter and audience versus competitors/past performance/future/etc." They are there to learn from us and to move forward with their newly received knowledge. In truth, they're there to help you as well, and keep in mind that most people know what it's like to be in your shoes and are naturally sympathetic.

Now that we've established the reality of the audience's role, we can act accordingly. We must prepare as if we are helping the audience. You are helping them to understand content and to accomplish their tasks in their respective roles. Even when you are persuading them via your presentation, you're fundamentally helping them to support you. Any way you look at it, you are helping the audience. This is the optimal mindset for a presenter to adopt heading into their presentation.

Helpful Analogy

Imagine yourself walking along the sidewalk of a busy street. You see an elderly person on the ground struggling to get up, using their cane as a support as they strain to erect themselves, but can't. Your instinct would be to reach out and help the person up. Think about that for one moment. You would not likely be concerned with how many people are watching you, or what they're evaluation of you is. You really wouldn't even consider what the elderly person is thinking of you. You would be focused on helping that person. When you are genuinely trying to help someone, you are not nervous. Therefore, to curb your nerves, shift your focus to helping your audience understand your content. For best results, consider approaching your professional presentation in this way. In all of my experience and research as a Presentation Specialist, I have yet to see this strategy fail to improve a presentation.

Micro Strategies

- **Rationalize** - Recognize that everyone has some presentation anxiety, even professional speakers
- **Take your time** - As presenters in a professional setting, we are three times (3x) more impatient with ourselves than others are with us. This means that when we pause to collect our thoughts, we do not need to rush to speak. If we feel that we have to continue on in two seconds, the audience will comfortably bear with us for six[3]
- **Manage your breathing** - Breathing is the most effective technique to override your adrenaline when it starts pumping. You cannot control your heart rate directly, but you can control your breathing, which indirectly impacts your heart rate. When you slow down your breathing, taking fewer, longer breaths, you will slow down your heart rate. This process will immediately help you refocus and regain control
- **Calculated deep breaths** - Start deep breathing about five minutes before you begin presenting. Inhale for six seconds, then exhale for eight seconds. It's beneficial to close your eyes and think of a pleasant memory or a relaxing vacation simultaneously. These combine to form a type of presentation meditation to help you deliver more effectively
- **Recalibrate breathing** - Continue controlling your breathing

throughout your presentation. This formula will put you back in the driver's seat when you anticipate feeling overwhelmed

- **Rehearse as often as possible** - Each rehearsal will improve your confidence. At minimum, you should be rehearsing at the specially designed times in this guide's framework. This effort will iron out any kinks in your delivery and weed out any unnecessary content. It's like beta testing, and it works

- **Perform mental repetitions** - While rehearsing or performing mental reps, run through the entirety of your presentation. Do not stop and restart when you've made a mistake. Continue on to the end. This process will prepare you to recover and proceed if/when mishaps occur live. You will feel more comfortable and perform better. This technique is used by Olympic downhill skiers; they avoid envisioning a perfect run every time because, if they falter, it will be more difficult for them to recover efficiently

- **Choose your attire in advance** - You'll be more comfortable and it will be one less thing to contemplate the day of your presentation

- **Arrive ahead of time** - As you would for a job interview. Remember that you may need time to set up your tech and prepare your environment

- **Befriend your audience** - In the event that you have some time to spare before your presentation, say hello and converse with those in the audience. This approach will build rapport while reducing your nervousness. You'll likely find that they can relate to you and are pleased to chat

- **Express positivity** - Smile and nod at the audience when possible. This gesture will prompt them to do the same and they will appear more friendly. In turn, you'll feel more comfortable

- **Hydrate** - Bring some water with you if you are prone to having a dry mouth. You can pause and take a sip when needed

- **Tactile comfort** - Holding a clicker, pointer, or pen has a

soothing effect and will help you to focus
- **Embrace pauses** - If you make a mistake or misspeak, take a moment to collect your thoughts, then continue
- **Eye contact hack** - When making eye contact, look at the spaces between individual audience members
- **Control the questions** - Consider asking your audience to hold their questions until the break or the end of your presentation. This decision will remove the fear of being caught off guard by a question and enable you to focus solely on presenting effectively
- **Use a disclaimer** - If you anticipate speaking too quickly and are concerned about it being perceived as nervousness or a lack of preparation, begin with a general statement to the audience informing them that you are very excited to present, and that if you end up speaking too quickly, invite them raise their hand to let you know. This pre-emptive approach will essentially disguise your nerves as excitement, which is more advantageous
- **Visualize engagement** - If your audience members are looking at their phones, you may be tempted to assume that they are not paying attention to your presentation. This concern will make it more difficult for you to present. Instead, presume that they are taking notes on what you are saying. This perception will encourage you to continue to deliver your content enthusiastically
- **Cultural awareness** - Lack of reciprocal eye contact may also have a cultural explanation. As mentioned previously, some cultures avoid eye contact as a sign of respect. Keeping this in mind will help you to continue presenting effectively

The Bright Side

The following statement about the delivery of a presentation is unmistakably true. When you're in front of your audience, just before you begin to speak, your presentation can go exceptionally well, or it can be a disaster, or it can fall anywhere in between. Focus on your desired outcome and presentation goals that you've carefully planned as you present. This focus will improve your probability of success. Consider the following: Imagine that there are two 10-year-old children, one on either side of a street. They are both tasked with walking 15 yards while balancing an egg on a spoon.

Child A is thinking: "I must get to the 15-yard mark smoothly."

Child B is thinking: "I must not drop this egg."

Which one do you think is more likely to cross the 15-yard mark with their egg intact? If you focus on the negative, you'll be drawn into it, like a suction or gravitational pull. The same is true of the positive. So, focus on your goal or desired outcome.

Utilizing Presentation Notes

You'll likely have notes, either in hard copy or available on your screen. Ideally, you'll have two sets of notes; one will be an overview of your presentation content, and the other made up of the excess information and content that you removed during your content selection. These can be used as a reference while presenting. Think of your notes as a handrail for going up or down the stairs. You will likely not need them all of the time, but if you lose your balance, they will be there to help you recalibrate and get back on track. Your presentation notes should be viewed in this way.

Remember that you're the person who will be the conveyer of knowledge. The moment when a presenter comes into their own is when they realize that their presentation is an opportunity to showcase their expertise and level of preparation. They tend to step up and engage with the audience as they are proud of their preparation. They have awaited this opportunity to demonstrate their knowledge and value to their organization. Be patient because sometimes, this takes exposure and repetition, but rest assured success will come. In the meantime, you will appear prepared, composed, and professional.

Chapter Eleven

Rehearsals, Going Virtual, & Final Send-Off

"Don't practice during performance"
– Mark Warriner

Rehearsal Benefits

Rehearsals are supremely important when it comes to professional presentations, yet due to time constraints and other issues, many executives either limit their rehearsal time or cut it out completely. They're similar to the stretching component of a workout: we all know it's valuable, yet it's often first to be cut when time is an issue. The prevailing rehearsal experience is for the presenter to review their slides one at a time the day before their presentation while talking to themselves. They say phrases such as: "Okay, here I'll explain our Unique Selling Proposition. Then, here I'll talk about the market trends." They basically assume that the right words will come to them in real time, as they present. Unfortunately for them, oftentimes the correct language and verbiage elude them in their moment of need and they struggle to find the right words on the fly. As you can imagine, it's quite difficult to scroll through your mental vocabulary while standing in front of an audience that's waiting on you to finish your thought. Furthermore, it's a direct pathway to hesitation, many "uhs" and "ums," extended pauses, and poor delivery.

The good news is that you can avoid this situation with very little effort by being proactive. When you speak your presentation aloud before your big day, you're able to identify concepts and content that require precise wording. Then you're able to search for and select language that you feel comfortable with and clearly captures your point. When you're crafting a professional presentation, remember that your rehearsals act as beta testing to iron out any kinks.

Rehearsals enable you to...

1. Fine-tune your word choice and phrasing while delivering your content
2. Integrate literary devices such as, similes, metaphors, analogies, examples, etc., to assist you in outlining key concepts
3. Assess your overall presentation
4. Identify and rectify any issues
5. Build confidence in advance of your presentation

Before your first rehearsal, speaking out your entire presentation may seem like a daunting task. You might be thinking of all of the mistakes that you'll have to correct in all of the different areas of your presentation (i.e., word choice, body language, vocal projection, visual aids, content organization, etc.). However, you'll be shocked at how quickly and easily you can spot and resolve issues. Some of the more complex concepts may take some time to find the best word choice to explain to an uninformed audience, but the other areas in need of improvement will become clear, along with their resolution. Not to mention the muscle memory you develop in the process, which benefits your overall delivery. For this reason, it's time very well spent. It takes very little compared to other framework components, and yields big time results. It's the equivalent of spending $10 on a car wash before you sell your car and receiving $300 more for the car.

Phrasing and Word Choice Strategies

Since you are the expert on your presentation topic, you'll already have an understanding and some idea of how to convey certain content to your audience. However, there are a few strategies that you can incorporate into your presentation to increase your effectiveness. The first is to focus on explaining your content as accurately and clearly as possible. This task means reflecting on your word choice, and consider integrating more user-friendly synonyms or alternatives, if possible. Keep in mind your audience's vocabulary and knowledge base along with your verbiage and comfort level. Secondly, using words and phrases that rhyme tend to resonate more with the audience. Take the phrases "Vision drives decision" or "Meet and greet," for example. This strategy stems from childhood when many of us were conditioned to remember rhyming content such as, "An apple a day, keeps the doctor away" or the alphabet song. While rehearsing your delivery of key content, consider rhyming terms and phrases to improve retention amongst the audience. Finally, there is magic in threes. Psychologically speaking, many people resonate more with content separated into three parts. Think of Julius Caesar's "I came, I saw, I conquered." This example also benefits from parallel structure, but it has stood the test of time. There are also the three wise men from The Bible; "the good, the bad, and the ugly;" "lights, camera, action!" and many more. Consider compartmentalizing some content of your presentation into three parts. If you're able to rhyme them, even better!

Efficient Rehearsal

Time is an issue when you are preparing for your professional presentation, as it is likely a fixed date. And most of us have other roles and responsibilities to tend to in addition to preparing a presentation. Therefore, our time is limited and we should endeavour to make the most of it. As illustrated earlier (Chapter Ten, *Controlling Nerves & Reducing Anxiety*), rehearsal of your presentation content will lead to muscle memory and help to improve the flow of your delivery. Rehearsing your content aloud will help you to gain an understanding of how it will sound to the audience, which is optimal. However, a powerful substitute is performing mental reps. Many successful, world-class performers practice this technique with great results.[1] You can mentally rehearse your presentation at various points throughout your day. This process will improve your automaticity when delivering your presentation as it will feel more familiar and natural to you.

Effective Rehearsal

Rehearsing with a coach, confidant, or close colleague is always a valuable option. Of course, this exercise takes some time and coordination. It also takes trust and courage to take your presentation for a test drive with a possible critic. However, if you have the luxury of a trustworthy confidant, you should take advantage of it. Just make sure that you give them direction. So, ask them to pay close attention to your body language, tone of voice, structure, etc. This guidance will help them to provide you with more accurate feedback. They might benefit from making a simple T-chart on a sheet of paper and listing your *strengths* on one side, and *working points* on the other. You do not have to agree with everything they say, and try not to spend your energy contending with them. You can choose what to add, remove, or change. At the end of the day, your goal is to improve before your presentation. If they can provide you with even one insight that you can correct or implement to improve, the process will have been worthwhile.

Rehearsing in front of the mirror is an "old faithful:" a tried and true method of practice. The mirror enables you to assess yourself in real time while you deliver your presentation. The issue is that if you're assessing your delivery skills, you're more prone to lose track of your presentation. It's very difficult to master this method of practicing and assessing simultaneously. A more advanced and modern alternative is to record yourself with either your smartphone, tablet, or laptop while you are rehearsing. This way, you can focus on delivering while you're recording, then as you're viewing yourself, you can be more objective and make changes to improve your presentation. In fact, the best option would be to have a confidant observe and record you simultaneously. You can then review the recording together and collaborate on the best adjustments to make. When electrical engineers wire up a new building, they need to check to ensure that all of the circuits are functioning properly before they sign off. They have a simple method to test and troubleshoot their circuits. They fire them, identify the break, repair the break, then fire them again. Rehearsals in advance of presentations should be approached with this in mind.

Going Virtual

In this new, post-pandemic era, many organizations have adapted or have at least become more accepting of virtual professional presentations. Overall, virtual presentations adhere to the same framework and skills as outlined in this book; however, some aspects become less important while others are amplified. For example, some body language aspects like movement and eye contact become less important in a virtual presentation. The presenter is typically stationary and since the physical human element is removed, eye contact is unattainable. However other aspects such as word choice, verbiage, and using more descriptive language become amplified as they are more influential in improving the audience members' understanding. There are two delivery methods of virtual presentations: Synchronous and Asynchronous, which mean live and pre-recorded, respectively. Their attributes, advantages, and disadvantages are outlined below.

Synchronous Presentations

Many platforms such as Zoom, GoToMeeting, Microsoft Teams, WebEx, etc. offer video conferencing options, through which the presenter can share their presentation slides with attendees and deliver their content virtually. These platforms enable audience members to raise their hand, type in questions or comments, and speak if need be. Virtual presentations have the benefit of gathering many people from different locations simultaneously as well as them being able to type in their questions and concerns to communicate with the presenter. This opportunity can lead to better understanding and more clarity. However, the drawbacks are that the audience members still need to be available with internet access at the specified time, the presenter will not be able to read the audience's body language, the presenter may not be able to use their own body language, and then there's always the threat of technology malfunctioning. Additionally, to establish a smooth session and minimize distractions, kindly ask your audience members to mute their microphones. It's rather difficult to deliver a presentation effectively when you're hearing fans, beeps, and people chatting in the background. Consider having a moderator on standby to help streamline and filter any incoming questions or concerns. This strategy will help you to focus on your delivery, while being considerate of the audience. Also, occasionally bandwidth is an issue for people and they may turn their camera's off as a result. Be prepared to deliver to an empty screen, and make an effort to verbally check in throughout your presentation. Finally, forecasting content and outlining expectations are crucial when delivering a presentation virtually. I recommend preparing an opening script with instructions and details included to set the stage for your delivery.

Asynchronous Presentations

Many presentation programs such as Google Slides, PowerPoint, and Keynote, along with programs like Screencast and Camtasia, enable you to record your presentation slides with your voiceover. Some programs even allow for a visual of your face to be displayed alongside your visuals. These types of virtual presentations allow you to deliver your presentation, complete with your visuals, while focusing on your content and material. The benefits to this type of presentation are that you can record and rerecord as often as you'd like until you are pleased with the result. Secondly, since it is recorded, your audience can watch it at their convenience and as often as they'd like, which may improve comprehension and reception. The drawbacks are that there is no live questions and answer period available and you are not able to gage whether or not the audience has understood your content. Again, there is the threat of technology malfunctioning and your audience not receiving your presentation. To maximize effectiveness, consider scheduling a synchronous Q & A follow-up session to clarify any confusion and ensure understanding.

Final Send-Off

The final analogy that I offer in this guide is that of two people playing catch. There are three components to this analogy: the thrower, the catcher, and the object. The desired outcome is for the catcher to catch the object. The object represents your presentation. The more clear, organized, customized, and professional it is, the more likely the audience will oblige the presenter. It's the difference between throwing a large rock to someone as opposed to a beach ball. The thrower is the presenter. The better prepared they are, and the better delivery skills (word choice, vocal projection, body language, etc.) they have, the smoother the throw. The audience is the catcher. Understanding where they are in relation to the thrower, how far away they are, their level of catching ability, their preference of catching technique will improve the likelihood of a completed catch.

Understanding your audience, your content, and yourself are key. This knowledge will give you a delivery target and help you become more focused. Design your presentation to meet as many of your audience members' needs as possible. This information will help shape your presentation to become more appealing for your audience. Your presentation delivery will become smoother as a result. Forecast to your audience what they can expect, then deliver your content as you've prepared. From this perspective, your presentation will become less stressful and more effective.

Showtime

As a child, I was involved in a few team sports. Growing up in a small town, the parents of my teammates took turns coaching us over the seasons. My father had a simple motto when it came to sports and performing: "Don't practice during performance!" Meaning that development of your skills should be done beforehand in practice, not during game time. Your focus during your practice should be micro: developing and improving your skills that will help you to succeed. But your focus during performance should be macro: achieving or accomplishing your goal. Consider the following: Michael Jordan doesn't focus on developing his passing skills during game time; he focuses on winning the game. Go forth and conquer!

Chapter Twelve

International Presenters and Second Language Speakers

International Presenter Perspective

I have always had a tremendous amount of respect for international presenters and English as a second language (ESL) speakers. As a former Professor of English, I'm well aware of the challenges international speakers face leading up to their time on center stage. They have been tasked with presenting in another language to audience members who are native speakers of that language. This means that in addition to all of the traditional apprehensions that most presenters face, international presenters have added and amplified concerns. Many are concerned with their vocabulary size and that they will not be able to adequately express themselves in their moment of need. Or perhaps they'll misuse a term or phrase and not realize while the audience reacts questionably. Others have pronunciation concerns in that their audience won't be able to understand them, or worse, view them as being unintelligent. Some tend to feel enhanced vulnerability stemming from the environment and different culture. At the end of the day international presenters are likely to feel a heightened sense of nervousness. This all seemed extremely daunting to me and I have always admired their courage.

When I first became a Presentation Specialist and Coach, many of my first clients were international business professionals and ESL speakers. They have taught me so much in terms of culture and have forced me to innovate new approaches to different types of presentations. So, I felt compelled to dedicate a chapter of this guide to helping international presenters everywhere. May this guide be a resource to you before, during, and after your time in the spotlight.

Audience Perspective

Your audience will understand that it's not easy to present in front of peers, subordinates, superiors, or anyone for that matter. They are more concerned with how you handle yourself and perform during the presentation, than on any errors you might make. What's most important is that you showcase a high level of preparation and professionalism. Realize that most audience members will notice that you speak with an accent, and you may have made a grammatical error or two. But unless you stumble regularly, your audience's main take-away will be your message and professionalism, not your mistakes.

Set Yourself Up for Success

The professional presentation framework outlined in this guide was universally designed to accommodate all presenters in all circumstances. Ultimately, if you are an international presenter, consider investing more time on preparation and making yourself comfortable. If you've followed this guide and utilized the phrases included in each chapter, you'll be well prepared for your upcoming presentation. Additionally, I have amassed a number of considerations and words of advice for you, listed below...

Advice and Considerations

- **Choose your words carefully** - Understand the meaning of the words that you plan to use in your presentation, and how to pronounce them. If you're having pronunciation difficulty with a word or term, you should either replace it with a synonym, or practice to improve its pronunciation. This process will also boost your confidence
- **Control your pace of speaking** - Many international presenters tend to speed up their speaking when they are presenting and

their words begin to blend together. This confuses the audience and adds an extra cognitive load on them as they attempt to make sense of what you've said. It's better to mispronounce one word in a sentence than the entire sentence. Slow down and smile

- **Pronounce each word completely** - A mispronounced word is also far better than reducing syllables, which turns into mumbling. Mumbling is taxing on and frustrating to the audience, so prepare and deliver with confidence
- **Cut yourself some slack** - Avoid putting too much pressure on yourself to be perfect. I promise you right now, that you will make a mistake. In all my years of presentation experience, I have never seen a perfect presentation. Something will go wrong, and that's okay. Expect it, breathe, and move forward
- **Keep your composure** - Many international presenters become very robotic with their body language and gesturing when using visual aids. Lack of humanity detracts from your presentation's appearance. Try to remain calm and help the audience to understand what you already know
- **Don't force yourself** - You want to appear as natural as possible while maintaining your professionalism. Your body language and vocal projection should be automatic and natural to you. If you feel like you're forcing something, so will your audience. You should aim to be on the outer edge of your comfort zone. That's where you will thrive
- **Expand your comfort zone** - This development will likely occur during your rehearsal time. Rehearsals are extremely important to international presenters because you are creating a form of muscle memory for yourself and when the time comes for you to present, you'll be more comfortable and confident. You may find yourself being on autopilot but still able to emphasize content when necessary
- **Manage your breathing** - Leading up to your presentation. Focus on deep breathing and mentally relaxing yourself.

International presenters tend to have a high degree of stage fright, which can be crippling if you let it. Instead, breathe slowly in a controlled manner, and you will take back control

- **Smile often** - Smiling is your best friend in a presentation. When you smile, it will make you happier and cause your audience to smile back. When you see your audience members smile, you'll begin to calm and view them more as friends than enemies

- **Lose the script** - Many international presenters' default to reading or memorizing a script in advance of their presentation. The trouble with reading is that you will eventually lose your place and frantically scan to find it. Not to mention that your audience will likely be snoring or on their phones. If you attempt to memorize your script, you risk forgetting your memorization and being lost. And even if you do remember your script, you will likely sound unnatural and awkward. So avoid both by knowing your content and rehearsing

- **Avoid idioms and colloquial phrases** - These can be easily mixed up or misunderstood if used incorrectly. Instead, you might consider using an alternative phrase, or asking the audience for confirmation. This technique will prompt your audience members to help and become more engaged

- **Dress appropriately** - Much of your choice of attire will depend on your workplace and circumstances, but you should always lean more toward a professional wardrobe. When you're presenting internally, you should consider bringing a jacket with you to wear during your presentation. When presenting externally, you should consider wearing a suit

- **Use correct body language** - Body language differs among cultures. Eye contact and gesturing are encouraged in North American culture, so make an effort to try. There may also be gestures that are culturally inappropriate and considered offensive (recall Chapter Eight, *Body Language*). Be mindful

Acknowledgements

Upon reflecting on all of the individuals who have helped contribute to this book, I realize that this may be one of the more difficult sections of this book to write. There have been so many people willing to help, in a variety shapes and forms. I am truly blessed to have surrounded myself with such incredible people.

The contents of this book reflect the countless hours of observation, collaboration, and research of countless presenters over time. Before I go too far, this book would not have been possible but for the work of many scientists and researchers who have selflessly shared their findings with the world. Never more has Sir Isaac Newton's "Standing on the shoulders of giants" rang true.

Thank you to my late father who always supported me and my quest to help others. To my friend and brother, Gianni Vitucci, thank you for motivating me to take the first step in writing this book and for encouraging me throughout the process. A deep and special thank you to Ed Wu, for illuminating this path and giving me a nudge in the right direction now and again. And a special thank you to Drew Smith for always being there to review and discuss ideas.

I'd also like to extend my gratitude to Wajeeh Alvi for assisting with the visual aids and graphics. The *Professional Presentation Framework* is a masterpiece. Thank you to Gianluca Agostinelli for your assistance in proofreading and suggesting revisions to improve the quality of the book. Your suggestions have helped a great deal. Thank you to Alexander MacGregor for your efforts in proofreading and sharing your thoughts. They have helped to refine the lessons for readers. Thank you to Greg Higginbotham for assisting with the design and formatting of the supplemental material and resources. To Eric Migicovsky, thank you for your all of your advice and time you spent assisting me. The John Hunt Publishing team should also be recognized for their role in bringing this book to fruition and willingness to accommodate my requests. I greatly appreciate your efforts.

Finally, a very special thank you to Dr. Anna Moro for all of your support and mentorship. Your warmth and encouragement have been an inspiration to me.

About the Author

www.professionalpresentationservices.com

Ryan Warriner is the founder and Lead Presentation Expert of Professional Presentation Services. He is also a Presentation Specialist and Coordinator at McMaster University. With over a decade of Professional Presentation experience and expertise, Ryan has mastered the science and art of presentations. His systematically designed frameworks make even the most challenging of speaking events, manageable and straightforward. His proprietary presentation framework has garnered international praise and continues to help countless presenters.

His formal education includes degrees in both English and Psychology, as well as master's degrees in Education and Professional Education. Throughout his career, Ryan has performed thousands of professional presentations, while designing hundreds more. He has advised and coached a vast clientele that includes everyone from college students to corporate CEOs.

Follow Ryan and Professional Presentation Services on LinkedIn at:
www.linkedin.com/ryanwarriner
and www.linkedin.com/professional-presentation-services

Thank you for your interest in *The Effective Presenter*. My sincere hope is that you derived as much from reading this book as I have in creating it. If you have a few moments, please feel free to add your review of the book at your favourite online site for feedback. Also, if you would like to connect with other books that I have coming in the near future, please visit my website for news on upcoming books, events, and free resources: *www.professionalpresentationservices. com*.

Sincerely, Ryan J. Warriner

Notes

Introduction

1. Oden, G. C., & Massaro, D. W. (1978). Integration of featural information in speech perception. *Psychological review*, *85*(3), 172.
2. Lee, D., & Hatesohl, D. (1983). Listening: Our most used communication skill.
3. Harris, R. (1986). *The origin of writing* (p. 29). London: Duckworth.
4. Archaeological Institute of America (2016). https://www.archaeology.org/issues/213-1605/features/4326-cuneiform-the-world-s-oldest-writing
5. Nichols, J. (1998). The origin and dispersal of languages: Linguistic evidence. In Nina Jablonski and Leslie C. Aiello, eds., *The Origin and Diversification of Language,* pp. 127-70. (Memoirs of the California Academy of Sciences, 24.) San Francisco: California Academy of Sciences

Chapter Three

1. Kosslyn, S. M., Kievit, R. A., Russell, A. G., & Shephard, J. M. (2012). PowerPoint® presentation flaws and failures: a psychological analysis. *Frontiers in psychology*, *3*, 230.
2. Lund, A. M. (1997). Expert ratings of usability maxims. *Ergon. Des.* 5, 15–20.
3. Sweller, J., van Merrienboer, J. J. G., and Paas, F. G. W. C. (1998). Cognitive architecture and instructional design. *Educ. Psychol. Rev.* 10, 251–296.
4. Wolfe, J. M. (1998). "Visual search," in *Attention*, ed. H. Pashler (East Sussex: Psychology Press), 13–56.

Chapter Four

1. Kosslyn, S. M., Kievit, R. A., Russell, A. G., & Shephard, J. M. (2012). PowerPoint® presentation flaws and failures: a psychological

analysis. *Frontiers in psychology*, *3*, 230.

2. Whitler, K. (2018). Why Too Much Data Is A Problem And How To Prevent It. Forbes Media LLC. https://www.forbes.com/sites/kimberlywhitler/2018/03/17/why-too-much-data-is-a-problem-and-how-to-prevent-it/#2c09c2ba755f

Chapter Five

1. Karns, T. E., Irvin, S. J., Suranic, S. L., and Rivardo, M. G. (2009). Collaborative recall reduces the effect of a misleading post event narrative. *N. Am. J. Psychol.* 11, 17–28.

2. Wurman, R. S. (1997). Information architecture. *Lakewood: Watson-Guptill Pubns.*

3. Lund, A. M. (1997). Expert ratings of usability maxims. *Ergon. Des.* 5, 15–20.

4. Helander, M., Landauer, T., and Prabhu, P. (eds). (1997). *Handbook of Human-Computer Interaction*. New York: Elsevier Sciences.

5. Iacoboni, M. (2009). Imitation, empathy, and mirror neurons. *Annual review of psychology*, *60*, 653-670.

6. Goldstein, N. J., Martin, S. J., & Cialdini, R. (2008). *Yes!: 50 scientifically proven ways to be persuasive*. Simon and Schuster.

7. Greenberger, D., & Padesky, C. A. (2015). *Mind over mood: Change how you feel by changing the way you think*. Guilford Publications.

8. Ronningstam, E., & Baskin-Sommers, A. R. (2013). Fear and decision-making in narcissistic personality disorder—a link between psychoanalysis and neuroscience. *Dialogues in clinical neuroscience*, *15*(2), 191.

9. Seli, P., Risko, E. F., Smilek, D., & Schacter, D. L. (2016). Mind-wandering with and without intention. *Trends in cognitive sciences*, *20*(8), 605-617.

Chapter Six

1. Kosslyn, S. M., Kievit, R. A., Russell, A. G., & Shephard, J. M. (2012). PowerPoint® presentation flaws and failures: a psychological

analysis. *Frontiers in psychology*, *3*, 230.

2. Aspillaga, M. (1996). Perceptual foundations in the design of visual displays. *Comput. Human Behav.* 12, 587–600.

3. Vekiri, I. (2002). What is the value of graphical displays in learning? *Educ. Psychol. Rev.* 14, 261–312.

4. Buchel, C., Josephs, O., Rees, G., Turner, R., Frith, C. D., and Friston, K. J. (1998). The functional anatomy of attention to visual motion – a functional MRI study. *Brain* 121, 1281–1294.

5. Phillips, D. (2014). How to avoid death By PowerPoint. *TEDxStockholmSalon.* https://www.youtube.com/watch?v=Iwpi1Lm6dFo

6. Cowan, N. (2001). The magical number 4 in short-term memory: A reconsideration of mental storage capacity. *Behavioral and brain sciences*, *24*(1), 87-114.

Chapter Seven

1. Lockwood, T. (2008). Voice and language. Call centres: Maximising performance training manual. Fenman Professional Training Resources. http://www.fenman.co.uk/traineractive/training-activity/voice-and-language.html

2. Beare, K. (2020). How to Write a Business Report for English Learners. ThoughtCo, thoughtco.com/how-to-write-a-business-report-1210164.

3. CDC/National Center for Health Statistics. (2017). Life Expectancy. https://www.cdc.gov/nchs/fastats/life-expectancy.htm

Chapter Eight

1. Mehrabian, A. (1971). Silent messages. Belmont, CA: Wadsworth.

2. Tubbs, S., & Moss, S. (2006). Human communication: Principles and contexts. New York, NY: McGraw Hill.

3. Ekman, P. (2009). Lie catching and microexpressions. *The philosophy of deception*, *1*(2), 5.

4. Bowden, M. (2010). Winning body language. NY: McGraw Hill.

Chapter Nine

1. Brockhoff, K., Margolin, M., & Weber, J. (2015). Towards empirically measuring patience. *Universal Journal of Management, 3*(5), 169-178.

Chapter Ten

1. Nunes, k. (2020). Fight, Flight, Freeze: What This Response Means. *Healthline Media a Red Ventures Company.* https://www.healthline.com/health/mental-health/fight-flight-freeze

2. Grohol, J. (2018). What is Exposure Therapy?. *Psych Central.* Retrieved from https://psychcentral.com/lib/what-is-exposure-therapy/

3. Brockhoff, K., Margolin, M., & Weber, J. (2015). Towards empirically measuring patience. *Universal Journal of Management, 3*(5), 169-178."

Chapter Eleven

1. Bassham, L. (1995). With Winning in Mind. *Bassham.* USA.

BUSINESS
BOOKS

Business Books

Business Books publishes practical guides
and insightful non-fiction for beginners and professionals.
Covering aspects from management skills, leadership and
organizational change to positive work environments, career
coaching and self-care for managers, our books are a valuable
addition to those working in the world of business.

15 Ways to Own Your Future
Take Control of Your Destiny in Business and in Life
Michael Khouri
A 15-point blueprint for creating better collaboration, enjoyment,
and success in business and in life.
Paperback: 978-1-78535-300-0 ebook: 978-1-78535-301-7

The Common Excuses of the Comfortable Compromiser
Understanding Why People Oppose Your Great Idea
Matt Crossman
Comfortable compromisers block the way of anyone trying to
change anything. This is your guide to their common excuses.
Paperback: 978-1-78099-595-3 ebook: 978-1-78099-596-0

The Failing Logic of Money
Duane Mullin

Money is wasteful and cruel, causes war, crime and dysfunctional feudalism. Humankind needs happiness, peace and abundance. So banish money and use technology and knowledge to rid the world of war, crime and poverty.

Paperback: 978-1-84694-259-4 ebook: 978-1-84694-888-6

Mastering the Mommy Track
Juggling Career and Kids in Uncertain Times
Erin Flynn Jay

Mastering the Mommy Track tells the stories of everyday working mothers, the challenges they have faced, and lessons learned.

Paperback: 978-1-78099-123-8 ebook: 978-1-78099-124-5

Modern Day Selling
Unlocking Your Hidden Potential
Brian Barfield

Learn how to reconnect sales associates with customers and unlock hidden sales potential.

Paperback: 978-1-78099-457-4 ebook: 978-1-78099-458-1

The Most Creative, Escape the Ordinary, Excel at Public Speaking Book Ever
All The Help You Will Ever Need in Giving a Speech
Philip Theibert

The 'everything you need to give an outstanding speech' book, complete with original material written by a professional speechwriter.

Paperback: 978-1-78099-672-1 ebook: 978-1-78099-673-8

On Business And For Pleasure
A Self-Study Workbook for Advanced Business English
Michael Berman
This workbook includes enjoyable challenges and has been de-
signed to help students with the English they need for work.
Paperback: 978-1-84694-304-1

Small Change, Big Deal
Money as if People Mattered
Jennifer Kavanagh
Money is about relationships: between individuals and between
communities. Small is still beautiful, as peer lending model, micro-
credit, shows.
Paperback: 978-1-78099-313-3 ebook: 978-1-78099-314-0

Readers of ebooks can buy or view any of these bestsellers
by clicking on the live link in the title. Most titles are published
in paperback and as an ebook. Paperbacks are available in
traditional bookshops. Both print and ebook formats are
areavailable online.
Find more titles and sign up to our readers' newsletter at
http://www.jhpbusiness-books.com/
Facebook: https://www.facebook.com/JHPNonFiction/
Twitter: @JHPNonFiction